Multi-Sensory Bible

15 ready-to-use sessions to explore God's epic story –
for creative churches and groups

Terry Clutterham

MULTI-SENSORY BIBLE by Terry Clutterham

© Terry Clutterham
First published by Scripture Union 2012

ISBN 978 1 84427 621 9

Scripture Union, 207–209 Queensway, Bletchley, Milton Keynes, MK2 2EB, UK
email: info@scriptureunion.org.uk
website: www.scriptureunion.org.uk

Cover design: by Waldon, White and Jones

Internal layout: Andrew Clarke

Internal illustrations: John Batten

Printed and bound by Melita Press, Malta

Scripture Union is an international Christian charity working with churches in more than 130 countries.

Thank you for purchasing this book. Any profits from this book support SU in England and Wales to bring the good news of Jesus Christ to children, young people and families and to enable them to meet God through the Bible and prayer.

Find out more about our work and how you can get involved at:

www.scriptureunion.org.uk (England and Wales)

www.suscotland.org.uk (Scotland)

www.suni.co.uk (Northern Ireland)

www.scriptureunion.org (USA)

www.su.org.au (Australia)

Contents

For
Sue, Jane, Paul, Kim, Linda, Emma and Tina
Discoverers together

Making the most of Multi-Sensory Bible

Introduction

The Bible tells a true story of vast proportions – God's amazing saving plan. It's the story of how he creates all good things, and saves and shapes people to be his and to point others to him. The story encompasses the whole cosmos – all centuries, every nation, the lives of hundreds of thousands of Bible characters, and billions more people ever since, and on into the future. Epic plan.

Then there are the present, extraordinary lives of people like Jo, Matt, Edith, Mick, Tasha, Zac, us... These lives too have casts of thousands, breathtaking backdrops from all over the world, and accounts of thrilling, heroic deeds. Epic lives. Then again, much of it seems more ordinary.

By faith in Jesus, our epic lives can be part of God's epic plan. The purpose of Multi-Sensory Bible is to help us learn more about playing our role in it to the full.

Along the way we may experience comfort and discomfort, laughter and tears, challenge and affirmation, joy at the similarities between the good-news story we encounter in the Bible and the reality of our own good-news lives, and sorrow at the less-than-good-news differences. We need to accept all these experiences as God's work in us as he shapes us up for the unique part we will play in his epic.

Making 'multi-sensory' approaches count

People learn in many different ways. Some of us take things in simply by listening to someone speaking, but most struggle to do so. They need to see or taste or smell or touch, if they are to learn and if their learning is to be memorable for them.

In your group you'll have a mix of people and therefore a range of learning preferences. It's up to you as leader to get to know your group members well enough to understand how they prefer to learn, and then to tailor the variety of learning experiences so that there's always something for everyone. Be careful not just to use your own favourite learning approach all the time!

Read carefully through all the activities in each Bible session before deciding which to choose – don't just go for those you like the look of straight away, or that are the easiest to prepare!

Choosing sessions

The aim of the book is to help us grasp the big picture and whole story of the Bible, so it's hard to see which sessions could be left out! Plan to cover all 15 sessions, but maybe not all at one stretch. You could split the material into Old Testament (Sessions 1–9) and New Testament (10–15), with a break in the middle to do something different. Alternatively, break the pattern of a week-by-week approach by going away together for an overnight retreat, during which time you could cover perhaps two or three sessions and intersperse them with other activities.

The sessions in **Multi-Sensory Bible** follow a common 'menu' approach:

 ## Getting connected (allow 10–15 minutes)

There is usually a choice of two or three activities in this section. This icebreaker will get everyone involved and sharing together from the very beginning. It will also connect them to the overall theme of the session. Maybe you could have refreshments during this time too.

 ## Living Scripture (allow 40–45 minutes)

There may be a choice of two or three activities in this section. Select one or more according to the needs of your group members. Everyone will need to be able to see a Bible. Since all Scripture is 'God-breathed', you can expect God to speak to group members during this time with challenges, encouragements, new insights and prompting to change.

The resource pages you print out will use the New International Version (NIV), but it won't matter (and it may enhance your learning together) if group members come with different Bible versions.

 ## Touching God (allow 15–20 minutes)

Your group members will be encouraged to use their senses to reflect on what they have just heard from God or to explore it further. Perhaps they will even want to spend the time responding to God personally about what he has shown them.

 ## Reaching out (allow 15–20 minutes)

It's easy to skip over this part of the session, particularly if an earlier part has run on too long. A group that stops looking outwards will soon become stagnant. In fact, one important message from the whole Bible is that God is reaching out to those who don't yet know him. So 'Reaching out' often includes an idea for a social activity as a great way of drawing new people into the group. Plan one into your programme from time to time.

 ## Digging deeper

This section includes activities for your group to tackle between sessions, either to go further with what you have just discovered together, or to help them get ready for the next session.

1 Oh yes!
Creation

Genesis 1,2; Psalm 8; 104:1–15,24,25; John 1:1–5; Colossians 1:15–20

'In the beginning God created…' (Genesis 1:1). These five words say it all. Life, people, everything had a beginning, from the dark nothingness that reigned. But God was there before this time, and made everything. The Bible emphatically answers the question 'who?', not 'how?' nor 'why?' All that exists came from the Creator and reveals something of his nature. If we look carefully and wonderingly at creation, we catch a glimpse of God himself.

And how did God do it? He just said the word (Genesis 1:3,6,9,11,14,15,20,24,26) and everything sprang to life. By his word he created order, beauty and light, from chaos and darkness; he is the King of creation with all sovereignty, power and authority, making everything in relationship and harmony with everything else, including people.

Pray that you and your group will know the power of God's Word as you explore the Bible together over the coming sessions. Ask him to show you how you can gain (or regain) a sense of order, beauty and light in your own lives, and join in with the good, creative work he is still doing in the world.

 ## Getting connected

Making it good

A few days before the session, ask some or all of the group members to bring along something that will enhance the life of the group. For instance, they could bake a fabulous cake, or choose some original, creative music; buy superior coffee, or offer a small gift for everyone; arrange some flowers, or bring a piece of intriguing artwork. Just as God created everything from nothing, and saw that it was good, try to create a group environment that's second to none! Without being patronising, mention the fabulous quality of everything everyone brings.

OR

One big story

Which was your favourite story as a child? Why do you think that was?
Which is your favourite story, play or film now? Why?
Why do you think your choice has changed since you were a child?
What kind of story now gets you most engrossed in it? Why?

Explain that even though we may know lots of the individual stories from the Bible, with Multi-Sensory Bible, we'll discover that the Bible is all one big story … and we won't just get engrossed in it but discover we're part of it!

 ## Living Scripture

You will need: a range of different-coloured permanent felt markers; seven different-coloured balloons (see below, and maybe get two of each colour in case some burst!); enough Bibles for everyone to see one.

Distribute the balloons round the group. If you have more than seven people, some can pair up; if fewer than seven, give more than one balloon to some group members.

Everyone blows up their balloon. It represents a day of creation. They should read the relevant Bible verses (see below), write a big day number on their balloon with a marker, and then draw on their balloon their unique interpretation of what has been created on that day (see below).

> Yellow balloon: Day 1; Genesis 1:3–5; light
> Blue: Day 2; 1:6–8; sky
> Green: Day 3; 1:9–13; land, plants
> White: Day 4; 1:14–19; moon, sun, stars
> Red: Day 5; 1:20–23; sea creatures, birds
> Pink or brown: Day 6; 1:24–31; animals, people
> Cream: Day 7; 2:1–3; rest

They should also write, in a different colour, what they think their Bible verses tell us about who God is and what he is like. If God says, does, creates, thinks this, what can we say about him?

When everyone has finished, they should show their balloon, and describe what their verses tell them about God. How do the different days compare?

Tie the balloons in a bunch and hang them up until Session 2.

 Touching God

Creation meditation
You will need: the music someone brought for 'Making it good', or other lively, creative music; play dough (see recipe on the website or just buy some!).

Play the music. Give everyone some play dough. Ask them to make a model of themselves, either just their head and shoulders, or their whole body.

As they sculpt themselves, read the following Bible verses over the music, twice: Genesis 1:26,27; 9:6; Psalm 8.

Pause afterwards, and invite everyone to thank God for making people like us in his image (Genesis 1:26,27), 'a little lower than the heavenly beings'.

Keep the models together somewhere visible as a group, through all the sessions.

Jesus praise
The Bible assures us that it was by his Word – through Jesus – that God created everything. Jesus was with God before everything was created, and was the prime motivator of creation.

Together read John 1:1–5, Colossians 1:15–20 and 2 Peter 3:5–7, allowing the verses to stimulate your imagination about those times of creation. Then create a poem of praise by each in turn thinking of a descriptive line about creation and everyone joining in with a response to Jesus after it. Go round the group until your creativity dries up. For example:

> *When the first cold flash of light burst through the deep, swirling darkness,*
> *Jesus, through you and for you was all this made. Lord of creation, we praise you.*
> *When the first fresh green shoots burst from the barren, dusty earth,*
> *Jesus, through you and for you was all this made. Lord of creation, we praise you.*
> *When...*

Reaching out

Where's the most beautiful place, maybe the highest point that you could get to in a day? Invite a few of the group's friends, create a picnic that's full of colour and good for you (so no cream cakes!), and go to your selected place. Get everyone to take some photos showing the group having fun, and also some that reflect each of the six days of creation – the light, sky, plants, sunshine, birds, animals, people, and the group simply relaxing together. Enjoy, and if the moment is right, talk about God creating everything good and about him being King over all.

Start a Facebook group or Flickr account for the group, and upload all the photos, encouraging group members to comment. If it's a Facebook group, everyone could use it before the next session to log their thoughts and reflections. Invite any friends who came on the picnic trip to join the group, so that they can see what's going on too, session by session, and perhaps be enticed to join in.

 Digging deeper

You will need: copies of the resource sheet on page 10 or downloaded from www.scriptureunion. org.uk/msbible.

In Multi-Sensory Bible, we'll be looking for eight key actions of God that run all the way through the Bible (see page 10). The Bible is essentially the story of God – wherever we look in it, God is helping us to know what he's like, but primarily in the person of Jesus. There are of course plenty more actions of God in the Bible, but group members will have to look for these themselves.

Give everyone a copy of the journal sheet. (Each A4 copy will do for two sessions.) Tell them the Bible references of the passages you have used this session, and add Genesis 2:4–25. They should write them in at the top of their sheet.

Invite them to revisit the Bible passages covered in this session and reflect on which attributes of God were demonstrated where. They should note these in the space, and then answer the two questions:

How is God doing these things in my life and around me?

How might I become more like God in these ways, joining in with his work in the world?

Let everyone know that you'd like them to return next time and, as far as they're happy to, be ready to tell the others in the group what God has been saying to them.

Multi-Sensory Bible Journal

Session ☐

Bible passages

God...	Where in the Bible verses?	My life
		How is God doing these things in my life and around me?
creates		
provides		
shapes and leads		
forgives		
saves/rescues		How might I become more like God in these ways, joining in with his work in the world?
judges		
promises		
reveals who he is		
other		

2 Oh no!

The fall

Genesis 3

It wasn't long before the 'good' and the 'very good' that God created got spoilt. People had been created in God's image, and with this came dignity, an obvious uniqueness, and a close relationship with God. They had responsibility for the world, and an accountability to God for how they lived, for they also had freedom to choose (Genesis 1:26–28).

Sadly, Genesis 3 tells how people got way above themselves, using their freedom to go their own way rather than God's. The results of this were catastrophic, bringing the 'death' that God had promised if they disobeyed him. Not only people, but all creation paid the price, 'groaning as in the pains of childbirth' (Romans 8:22). It's often called 'The fall' – from innocence to guilt, from perfection to brokenness, from closeness to God to distance from him.

This isn't a happy subject to explore with your group, but pray that they'll find it helpful to reflect on the nature of sin, the serious consequences of the first people's disobedience, and the extraordinarily powerful grace of God.

 Getting connected

Sharing journals

Chat about what any individuals discovered as they wrote their 'journals' after last time. Invite people to contribute, but don't put people on the spot in case they haven't done it! What themes did they spot in Genesis 1 and 2, and where are those themes being played out in their own lives?

OR

Tempting!

You will need: a fruit bowl; a mixture of ordinary and unusual fruit; a knife; a chopping board; some paper napkins.

Prepare a mouth-wateringly tempting bowl of fruit and place it in the middle of the group. Make sure there are some exotic fruit, including some that people might not recognise.

Ask each group member in turn which of the fruits they are most tempted by, and why. Then invite everyone to try part of a fruit they have never tasted before. Chop some of the fruit in pieces and share it round.

 Living Scripture

You will need: slips of paper; pens; Bibles; last session's balloons; large sheets of paper.

If you did 'Living Scripture' last session, take a look at your bunch of balloons now. See how many times you can go round the group finding one difference each between the balloons when they were first blown up and the balloons now: 'Before, the balloons were …, but now they're …'

Laws of physics have kicked in to spoil things. When people made the wrong choice and decided to go their own way instead of obeying God, the whole of creation – and especially their relationship with God – was spoilt.

Read out Genesis 3:1–7.

Now encourage the group to listen for everything that was spoilt in God's good creation because of the man and woman's disobedience to him, starting with their sense of shame (v 8). Give everyone a pen and some paper to jot them all down. Read Genesis 3:8–24 slowly to the group. The group can follow in their Bibles, if they like.

Now ask the person to your left to read out their list. If anyone else has noticed the same things, they should tick them on their list. Then move on to the second person who only reads out anything that hasn't been ticked. Keep going round the group until everything has been said. If later you plan to do 'Today's news', write each suggestion on a separate, large sheet of paper as you go.

All this could be described as part of the 'death' God promised the man and woman for eating the forbidden fruit (v 3). The worst kind of 'death' is being cut off from God for ever. And all because the tempter questioned God's word, and the man and woman rejected God's authority.

But right at this point of judgement, God gives people the first hint of good news to come (v 15) – the good news of Jesus, the winner in the Christ versus Satan conflict. This is God's way – judgement and the amazing grace of God go hand in hand all the way through the Bible.

 Touching God

Poems
You will need: paper and pens; ambient music; the poem called 'I' downloaded from www.scriptureunion.org.uk/msbible.

No one has to be a poet to do this activity! It's about starting a thought and seeing where it takes us. Print out the poem called 'I' from the website. It's one the author wrote on a car journey thinking about the fall and Romans 3:23 (as often happens, of course!). Invite everyone to grab a space, put on ambient music and let them follow their thoughts and write. Maybe after a few minutes someone will have something they're able to share with everyone.

Today's news
You will need: everyone's smart phones (if they have them); alternatively, a laptop connected to the internet and open at a current news page; the large sheets of paper from 'Living Scripture'; markers; a copy of the resource sheet on page 14 for each group member or downloaded from www.scriptureunion.org.uk/msbible.

Grab the large sheets and place them around the room. Give everyone time to search on their phones for news items, or do it together on your laptop, and to think how they might relate to the brokenness you have listed on all the sheets. They can take a marker and write the headline for each news story on the appropriate large sheet.

When everyone has exhausted their news items, give them a copy of the resource sheet and invite them to think about which relationships are damaged in those stories. They can write the headline in the most appropriate segment and then use their sheet to pray for the world after this session.

Reaching out

Unlike the picnic spot you may have chosen last time, think of a neglected place that the group members could have fun fixing up. This could be a church member's garden or home, or a garage clear-out; in the community it could be a graffiti-wrecked wall, or some other eyesore – though of course you'll need to get the council's permission before you do anything in a public space, and be aware of potential health and safety issues.

This is just the kind of activity that would be good for group members to invite their friends to – relaxed, non-threatening, fun, mucking in as part of a team, and maybe a few light refreshments afterwards.

While you're working, encourage your group members to pray silently for the friends who have joined them and for the community you're part of. Cry out to God in your heart for any brokenness to be mended, especially any lost relationship with him.

Digging deeper

Multi-Sensory Bible journals

You will need: copies of the resource sheet on page 10 or downloaded from www.scriptureunion. org.uk/msbible.

If your group seems to have enjoyed and benefited from doing their journals last time, reissue the sheets and give them the Bible passage to fill in at the top – Genesis 3. They simply repeat the same theme-based activity again. If they didn't enjoy it, let them try something else!

As part of their reflection, encourage group members to take photos of parts of God's creation that really aren't as they should be. Then they can upload them to the group's Facebook group or Flickr account, if you have one.

Noah nuances

As an alternative to the journal activity, invite your group members to read or listen to the story of Noah (Genesis 6:1 – 9:17). Then they should depict visually, using any medium they like, two of the intertwining themes from Genesis 3 that they find in it – judgement and the saving grace of God. Where can they see these same two themes in the Noah story?

If you have any avid readers in the group, encourage them to purchase a copy of *The Oncoming Storm* by Andrew R Guyatt, published by Scripture Union 2011. It's a graphic, gripping retelling of the story of Noah, available from your local Christian bookshop or direct from Scripture Union at www.scriptureunion.org.uk/shop. Perhaps they would like to choose a passage from it that demonstrates these two themes, to read to the group next time you meet, or in a few sessions' time.

Today's News

1 From the list of news items you have gathered as a group, write each of the items in the appropriate segment below.

2 Now look at each segment and turn the bad news into prayers of sorrow and repentance on behalf of yourselves and the whole world.

A world of brokenness...

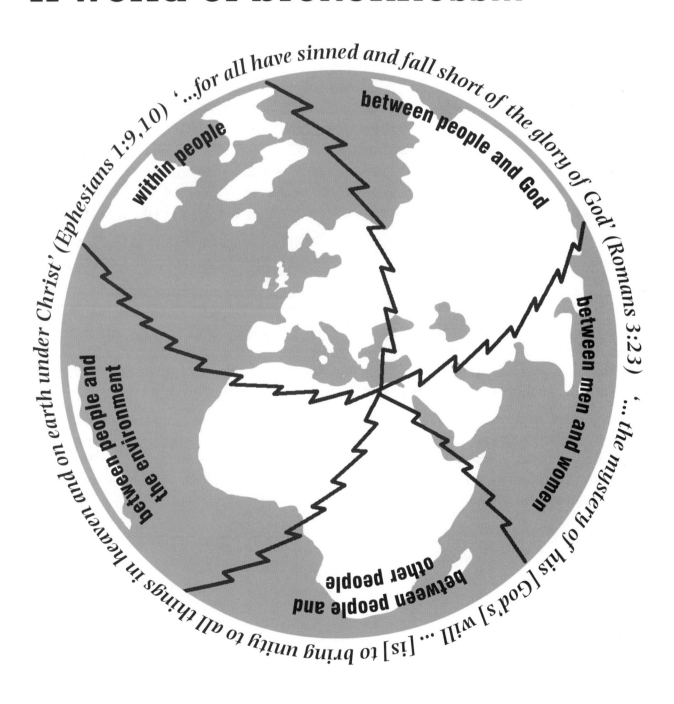

'...for all have sinned and fall short of the glory of God' (Romans 3:23) '...the mystery of his [God's] will ... [is] to bring unity to all things in heaven and on earth under Christ' (Ephesians 1:9,10)

within people

between people and God

between men and women

between people and other people

between people and the environment

3 Setting off

Abraham

Genesis 12:1–9; Hebrews 11:8–12

The years had moved on since Adam and Eve's false step with the forbidden fruit. Evil had firmly taken root in the world. What went wrong in the Garden of Eden stayed wrong – people seeking knowledge, wisdom and power without reference to God. Those who planned the doomed tower of Babel (Genesis 11:1–9) said, 'Come, let us build ourselves a city, with a tower that reaches to the heavens…' (v 4) – 'us', 'ourselves', the 'i' at the heart of 'sin'.

Only a few stayed true to God – for instance, 'Enoch walked faithfully with God 300 years' (Genesis 5:22), 'Noah found favour in the eyes of the Lord' (6:8), and God found Noah's family 'righteous' (7:1). But none of this earned them any special favours from God – God simply chose them to play a part in his future plan. He intended to bring back everything – including people – into a right relationship with himself and with each other. And how he did it is what the rest of the Bible story is all about!

Pray that your group will begin to grasp not only how important Abraham's part in God's plan was, but also their own part.

 Getting connected

Sharing journals

As before, chat about what any individuals discovered as they wrote their 'journals' after last time. Again, don't pressurise people to speak if they don't want to! What themes did they spot in Genesis 3, and where are those themes being played out in their own lives?

OR

Noah nuances

This activity follows on from 'Noah nuances' in Session 2, page 13. If anyone has depicted the themes in the Noah story they explored, invite them to show the group what they have created and, if necessary, to explain the thinking behind it. You could keep their creation in the room where you meet, since you'll keep coming back to these two themes all the way through the Bible.

Also, if anyone has read *The Oncoming Storm*, get them or someone else to read out an excerpt that demonstrates the themes of judgement and the saving grace of God.

The Bible in 50 words

You will need: the resource sheet on page 19 or downloaded from www.scriptureunion.org.uk/msbible; optional paid-for video version of 'The Bible in 50 words' by Ignitermedia from www.worshiphousemedia.com

The resource sheet outlines the whole story of the Bible in 50 words. Encourage your group to learn it by heart! But relax – you only need to work on the first four lines this time. Have fun! Distribute copies of the sheet to everyone to keep in their Bibles for reference.

Living Scripture

You will need: the 'Promises and obstacles' cards on page 18 copied or downloaded from www.scriptureunion.org.uk/msbible, and cut up; around 50 medium-sized stones (the washed, ornamental kind you find in garden centres).

Explain the following to your group:

The story since last time: Sin has entered the world, and everyone and everything suffers. God sent Adam and Eve away for disobeying him, though he still provided clothing for them. The relationship between God and people has broken down. Consequently human conflict is rife, as the story of Cain and Abel shows – brother even killing brother. But as well as judging him for his wickedness (Genesis 4:11,12), God shows mercy to killer Cain (4:15). The flood was God's judgement on sin, but the boat was God's saving grace in action. Sin couldn't overcome God's grace; God's love was still in action. This is the repeated story through the whole Bible. Things aren't right between God, creation and people – the rest of the Bible explains how God makes things right again.

Bring on the pile of stones. Explain that you're going to construct an altar – just a pretend one, of course! Abraham often built an altar at which to worship God and call on him (Genesis 12:7,8; 13:4,18; 22:9). Distribute the stones evenly around your group members.

First read aloud Genesis 12:1–3, the first time God made a promise to Abram – and what a promise! Together, place about 15 stones in a heap as the start of your 'altar'. Stick card 1 into the top of the stones so that it stands up. Also place on there any of the four 'Covenant promise' cards that relate to those verses.

Of the numbered pairs of cards, card 'a' verses demonstrate an obstacle to God's promise being realised, whilst card 'b' shows what God said in response. For each pair of cards:

● Together build up the 'altar' with a few more stones.

● One person reads out the Bible verses referenced on card 'a' and you discuss what the obstacle was.

● Someone else reads God's promise on card 'b', in response to the situation.

● Work out which of the four 'Covenant promise' cards relate to God's promise on card 'b', and pick up any new ones, if necessary.

● Stick the pair of cards and any new 'Covenant promise' cards into the 'altar'.

● Carry on building, picking up the next pair of cards. Repeat the same process until all the cards are stuck in the 'altar'.

Abraham had to learn to live by faith in God's promises, and in the fact that there was something far bigger going on than he could possibly imagine.

Touching God

Pass the globe

You will need: an inflatable globe small enough for people to pass round but large enough to read the country names easily. (These can be bought at low cost from Amazon.)

This prayer activity will keep everyone on their toes! Remove any breakable ornaments first, and then begin to throw the globe gently from one person to another. When they catch it, they should read out the name of whichever country is facing them and then find out from the group if anyone knows anything about it. If not, it doesn't matter. The person with the globe then leads the group in prayer for that country, asking God to touch those people with his love and to bring those who don't know him into a close relationship with himself.

 Reaching out

Go for a night walk together and see if you can see any stars. Go somewhere away from the bright street lights. Invite some friends along, especially anyone who knows anything about stars. It may help to download a stargazing app for your phone to help you identify the constellations. At some point, challenge everyone to begin counting the stars. (Don't take too long about it – just in our own Milky Way there are around 200 billion!)

 Digging deeper

Multi-Sensory Bible journals

You will need: copies of the resource sheet on page 10 or downloaded from www.scriptureunion. org.uk/msbible.

This time, reissue the sheets and give them the Bible passage to fill in at the top – Genesis 12:1–9 and Hebrews 11:8–12. Get them to write in this thought-starter at the bottom of the sheet:

'We're not Abraham, and this is around 4,000 years on. God hasn't given us the same part as Abraham to play in his plan of salvation for the world. But he has definitely given us a part in it. Talk with him about how you can play your part in it to the full.'

Then they can do the usual theme-based activity again.

A life of faith

The Genesis account of Abraham's life picks up the story when he is 75 years old! It's never too late to set out on the journey of faith. Encourage the group to read what we know of Abraham's life story in one sitting, from Genesis 12 to 25. It should take around an hour. They should keep in mind (and maybe jot down some answers to) these questions:

How would you describe the God who speaks and acts through these chapters?

What are some of the characteristics of the person of faith?

OBSTACLES AND PROMISES

Covenant promise

Descendants becoming a
great nation

Covenant promise

Descendants possessing the
Promised Land

Covenant promise

Descendants being God's
own people

Covenant promise

All peoples of the world being
blessed through Abraham

1 PROMISE **Genesis 12:1–3**	

2a OBSTACLE **Genesis 13:8–13**	**2b** PROMISE **Genesis 13:14–18**
3a OBSTACLE **Genesis 15:1–3**	**3b** PROMISE **Genesis 15:4–6**
4a OBSTACLE **Genesis 15:7,8**	**4b** PROMISE **Genesis 15:12–21**
5a OBSTACLE **Genesis 16:1**	**5b** PROMISE **Genesis 17:1–21**
6a OBSTACLE **Genesis 18:1–15**	**6b** PROMISE **Genesis 18:16–19**

The Bible in 50 words

God made
Adam bit
Noah arked
Abraham split
Jacob fooled
Joseph ruled
Bush talked
Moses baulked
Pharaoh plagued
People walked
Sea divided
Tablets guided
Promise landed
Saul freaked
David peeked
Prophets warned
Jesus born
God walked
Love talked
Anger crucified
Hope died
Love rose
Spirit flamed
Word spread
God remained

Source unknown

4 The shape of rescues to come
The plagues, the Exodus and the parting of the Red Sea

Exodus 6:1–8; 10:1–20; 11:1–10, 12:29–42; 14:10–31

Abraham held on to God's covenant promises by faith – everything that God had said would happen must have seemed highly unlikely! Several hundred years later, with Abraham's descendants in slavery in Egypt, it must all now have looked impossible, the Promised Land not even a speck on the far horizon.

Abraham's great-grandson, Joseph, had settled in Egypt with his father and brothers. Their descendants had grown into a huge nation, Israel. Around four hundred years later, 'a new king, to whom Joseph meant nothing, came to power in Egypt' (Exodus 1:8). Trouble brewed as the king surveyed the Israelites and felt his nation threatened. Slavery for the Israelite foreigners was the only solution.

However, through the life of Moses, the plagues, the Exodus and the parting of the Red Sea, God was about to demonstrate how nothing stands in the way of his promises and how rescue is at the heart of his plan for creation. His covenant people were definitely heading towards the Promised Land!

Pray for your group members individually. Ask God to help them see how the disappointments, disasters and setbacks in their daily lives and plans can be woven into his far greater plan, and used for good.

 Getting connected

Multi-Sensory Bible journals
As before, maybe over refreshments, chat about the reflections of those who have done the Bible journal activity. Recalling Abraham's life and journey, wonder together what it might mean for you to play your part in God's big plan.

OR

Rescues I have known
Ask if anyone can remember a time when someone rescued them out of a tight corner. What happened? How did they feel before they were rescued? Who came to their rescue? How did they feel afterwards?

The Bible in 50 words
You will need: a small, soft globe.

Learn by heart the next five lines of 'The Bible in 50 words'. Then add them to the first four lines that you learnt last time.

Have fun throwing the globe randomly around the group. Each time someone catches it, they have to say the next line without hesitation. Work out a small forfeit for anyone who misses their cue.

Living Scripture

You will need: a copy of the Bible timeline Part 1 from page 23 or downloaded from www.scriptureunion.org.uk/msbible; the three signs copied from the resource sheet on page 24 or downloaded from www.scriptureunion.org.uk/msbible; slips of paper; marker pens; Bibles.

Explain the following to your group, using the Bible timeline Part 1:

The story since last time: As Abraham looked up at the night sky, he must have wondered how all God had promised would come to be. He and Sarah had a son, Isaac, so things had started to look a bit more promising, but all peoples of the world being blessed through Abraham? At least the Promised Land wasn't that far away.

Isaac's son Jacob had twelve sons, including Joseph. Years passed by, and by a strange twist of history (but actually by the hand of God), they became happily settled in Egypt, all because of Joseph's rapid promotion to a prominent national position – prime minister. But 400 years later, Jacob and his sons had become a whole race of people, the Israelites. (Israel was another name for Jacob.) The Egyptian king didn't know anything about Joseph, and was worried about the huge number of 'foreigners'. To stop them overrunning Egypt, he made them slaves. God's appointed leader Moses couldn't persuade Pharaoh to let God's people go. The Promised Land must have seemed much farther away than ever before…

Spread the three signs on the floor across the room, with a pile of slips of paper and a pen nearby.

Divide the group into three teams. It doesn't matter if there's only one person in each team! Allocate each team to one of the three signs, and get them to sit by it. Each team will need a Bible.

Invite each team to use the Bible verses on their sign to answer the three questions. They should write each 'salvation' answer on one slip of paper, and each 'judgement' answer on another.

Finally, invite each small group to feed back their answers. Look together across all three parts of the rescue to see similarities and differences in your answers.

 Touching God

Multi-sensory memories
You will need: four small bowls; pitta bread; horseradish sauce; chutney or pickle; salty water; slices of lamb (or lamb curry).

When Jewish people remember these events in the celebration of Passover, they use multi-sensory reminders of the story. Do something similar. Prepare small bowls of each of the following, and pass them round in turn, inviting everyone to dip small chunks of pitta bread into them and taste it:

> Chutney or pickle = the mud used for making bricks
> Horseradish = bitter, harsh experiences
> Salt water = tears shed in slavery
> Lamb = God's act of salvation

As you pass each bowl round, say the appropriate sentence:

(Chutney/pickle) This looks like the mud for making bricks. Remember the struggles you've had in life.

(Horseradish) This is bitter. Remember the harsh things you've been through that have left scars on your life.

(Salt water) This tastes like tears. Remember the times you have cried recently.

(Lamb) This is lamb, like that killed at Passover. Remember the way God has rescued you from slavery to sin.

Smell of freedom
Ask everyone what they think of when you say the words 'smell of freedom'. What do they think the people of Israel would have said?

 ## Reaching out

Random pray-ers
Invite your group members to become random pray-ers. 'All peoples on earth will be blessed through you', God told Abram (Genesis 12:3). God wants everyone to experience and respond to his love. As random people come into your group members' lives over the next few days, they should pray silently for them to experience God's love in some way. They might be the people in front of them in the checkout queue, in the car behind them at the traffic lights, the work colleagues they find it hard to get on with, as well as their friends and family. God's love can reach anyone anywhere – random praying is fun. Like Abram your group members will possibly never see God's answers.

 ## Digging deeper

Multi-Sensory Bible journals
You will need: copies of the resource sheet on page 10 or downloaded from www.scriptureunion. org.uk/msbible.

If the journals are going well, reissue the sheets and give them the Bible passage to fill in at the top – Exodus 6:1–8; 10:1–20; 11:1–10, 12:29–42; 14:10–31. They can do the usual theme-based activity.

Bible timeline
Note the approximate date of the Exodus. Encourage a budding historian in the group to research what else was going on in the world around 1200 to 1300 BC. How similar or different was it to the situation in Egypt, with some people believing in the One True God?

Bible timeline Part 1

1300 BC
Moses

1240 BC
The Israelites enter the Promised Land

1630 BC
Jacob's family settle in Egypt

1760 BC
Jacob

1900 BC
Abraham

1280 BC
The Exodus

1700 BC
Joseph

1820 BC
Isaac

| 1900 BC | 1800 BC | 1700 BC | 1600 BC | 1500 BC | 1400 BC | 1300 BC | 1200 BC |

All dates are approximate

THE RESCUE

THE RESCUE PART 1
Exodus 6:1–8; 10:1–20

- In what ways does God act to save his powerless people? List each way on a slip of paper.
- Who or what does God judge by his actions? List each one on a slip of paper.
- In what other Bible events does God act to set his powerless people free?

THE RESCUE PART 2
Exodus 11:1–10; 12:29–42

- In what ways does God act to save his powerless people? List each way on a slip of paper.
- Who or what does God judge by his actions? List each one on a slip of paper.
- In what other Bible events does God act to set his powerless people free?

THE RESCUE PART 3
Exodus 14:10–31

- In what ways does God act to save his powerless people? List each way on a slip of paper.
- Who or what does God judge by his actions? List each one on a slip of paper.
- In what other Bible events does God act to set his powerless people free?

5 The only way is up
Wanderings and laws

Exodus 19:3–6; 20:1–17; Leviticus 9

So God's people were free from slavery, and heading for the land God had promised them. During this time, God constantly reminded them of his covenant with them – to be with them as their God, and they would in turn be his special people. They needed to obey him and allow their lives to be shaped to reflect his nature, so that all peoples on earth would be blessed because of them (Genesis 12:3). Usually they failed miserably at this, except, of course, through Jesus.

When God saves us from the slavery of sin, by faith in Jesus Christ, that's only the start of the work God wants to do in our lives. We set out on the road with nothing, but in faith and hope we gradually learn of God's faithfulness to his promises and how he wants us to live. Our horizon opens out from the world to the heavens and all eternity.

Our group members may be at many different points on their journey with God – just setting out, miles down the track, or almost at the end. Pray that through this session everyone will grasp both the privilege and the responsibility of being God's people in a world that is often hostile to them.

 Getting connected

Bible Journals and Bible timeline
Chat about the discoveries of those who have done the Bible journal activity. As they recall God's rescue of his people from slavery in Egypt, ask the group how free they feel they are spiritually.

If anyone did the research into what else was going on in the world around 1200 to 1300 BC, draw out the similarities and differences between those events and the story of the One True God rescuing his people from Egypt.

OR

Cupped hands
Bring to the group something you consider a treasured possession. Show it and explain why it is so special to you. Then invite everyone to cup their hands. Explain:

Imagine you have a treasured possession in your hands. Look at it closely. What's it made of? What colour is it? What makes it a treasured possession to you?

After a pause, introduce the reading by saying that after they had left Egypt, this is how God reminded his people of how much they meant to him. Read Exodus 19:3–6 aloud, preferably from the NIV, which includes the phrase 'my treasured possession'. Get everyone to open their hands.

Say:
I wonder if anyone has ever called you their 'treasure'. Well, God has, and still does. He looks at all his people and says, 'My own, my treasure'.

Living Scripture

You will need: a copy of the resource sheet 'God's rules' on page 28 or downloaded from www.scriptureunion.org.uk/msbible, printed on card and cut up; Bibles; pens.

Set the scene in this way:

The story since last time: Set free, God's people the Israelites journeyed towards the wonderful land God had promised them. On they trudged for two whole months until they arrived at the desert near a mountain called Sinai. The Israelites were about to discover that being God's 'treasured possession' meant loving him in return, living as his 'treasured possession' and showing what God is like to the rest of the world. While Moses was up the mountain, God gave him some special laws for the people, to guide them in living as the precious children of God that they now were…

Read Exodus 20:1–17 together.

Place the ten 'God's rules' cards in the centre of the group. (If you have a larger group, make enough sets of cards for every three or four people.)

Challenge everyone to sort the Ten Commandments into two groups: those that describe what God's people should be and do towards God, and those that describe what they should be and do towards each other.

For the commandments about attitudes and behaviour towards other people, what does each rule tell us about the nature of God? For instance, since God tells his people to respect their parents, he must love. Discuss in turn what each of the five rules reveals about God's nature.

But how could a holy God communicate with a sinful people who simply couldn't keep his laws? God's answer was the tabernacle – a tent of meeting. Here the priests would sacrifice bulls and rams as a sin offering and then, once purified, proceed into a tent where the Ark of the Covenant contained the two stone tablets containing the Commandments. Get volunteers to construct a tabernacle out of the ten cards – two for the tent in the centre and eight for the high fence around it.

As they do so, ask someone to read aloud Leviticus 9, which describes the tabernacle in action.

Discuss how you think the giving of the laws and the use of the tabernacle points to the good news of Jesus.

Each person should now take one of the ten cards and write on it where they have fallen short of God's standards by sinning. They should confess their sin silently, and then tear up their card, or burn it if you plan to do 'Burnt offering' (see page 27).

Touching God

Burnt offering

You will need: a fireproof container; matches.

Taking all appropriate safety precautions, encourage everyone to place their card in the fireproof container and then stand back. As you light the cards with a match, invite everyone to confess their sin to our holy God and pray that their lives will reflect him more and more each day.

Be holy

You will need: a bowl of warm water; soap; a towel; ambient music.

As well as burnt offerings, washing was a symbol of purification for the priests in the tabernacle (Exodus 30:17–21). Pass the bowl, soap and towel round the group, with each person washing their hands as a sign that they want to be clean of sin. As they do so, play the music and read Leviticus 11:44,45 as many times as necessary while the bowl does a complete circuit.

 Reaching out

Take the group camping for the night, and invite everyone to bring a friend. See how many tents the group members have, then maybe beg or borrow more from church. If the weather or the season isn't great for camping out, try camping indoors – in your church hall, village hall or local school. You could combine it with a meal-crawl around church members' homes, enjoying a starter in one home and then moving on for the main course, then dessert and finally drinks. This would be a great reminder of the nomadic life of the Israelites, and the fact that Christians don't really consider earth their home.

Remember to take photos and update the group's Flickr or Facebook pages.

 Digging deeper

Multi-Sensory Bible journals

You will need: copies of the resource sheet on page 10 or downloaded from www.scriptureunion. org.uk/msbible.

As usual, reissue the sheets and give group members the Bible passages to fill in at the top – Exodus 19:3–6; 20:1–17; Leviticus 9.

Random regulations

Invite group members to dip fairly randomly into the book of Leviticus. They should read some regulations that God gave his people about their lives, and then ask themselves what the regulations tell them about the nature of God. Group members could finish by exploring Leviticus 26:1–13, as a summary of what was going on between God and his people at this time. If the Israelites obeyed God, what promises would he fulfil?

GOD'S RULES

I am the only God	Don't murder
Do not worship idols	Be faithful in marriage
Respect my name	Don't steal
Have a weekly holy day (holiday)	Don't tell lies
Respect your parents	Don't be jealous

6 In too deep?

Jordan, Promised Land and judges

Deuteronomy 8:6–11; Joshua 14:1–5; 21:43–45; Judges 2:10–23; 10:6–16; 11:29–32; 21:25

Two spies, Joshua and Caleb, had gone into Canaan to survey the unknown territory. They returned to urge God's people to take his promises seriously and march boldly into the land. God would remain faithful to them. However, the people God had rescued from Egypt refused to enter the Promised Land and all died in the desert, except for Joshua and Caleb. As a result of this disobedience, the Israelites wandered in the desert for altogether 40 years on what should have been a few weeks' journey, and then died before they reached the longed-for destination. Only their children entered the land of God's promises.

Joshua was made leader in Moses' place. He and all the people stood on the east bank of the River Jordan waiting to cross into the land God had promised to give them – rather apprehensively, no doubt. Miraculously the water stood still – God was clearly at work, and his people could now cross over and take control.

But it wasn't long before they forgot about God and worshipped other gods. A cycle of faithlessness, disaster, despair, pleading and rescue became the norm for life in Canaan. Yet God's grace and faithfulness came through for them time and again, however undeserving they were.

Immediately we begin to see connections with our own life journey with God, and with Jesus. Pray that your group members will too.

 Getting connected

Promised Land snacks

You will need: coffee; a selection of bread; honey; pomegranates; grapes; olive oil; figs.

With the usual coffee and chat about journals, and about the 'Random regulations' activity from last time, have some 'Promised Land snacks' laid out. The menu is in Deuteronomy 8:7–10! The Israelites weren't getting all this because they were good, mighty, handsome or numerous, but simply because God chose them, and chose them because he loved them, and loved them just because he did (Deuteronomy 7:6–11). In return God wanted their wholehearted obedience to him.

OR

Invite everyone to share stories about the best food they have eaten in the best places on earth.

Google Earth

You will need: a computer or tablet; internet connection.

Ask group members to name their ideal place on earth to live and why they've chosen it. Open Google Earth and zoom in on the various countries or areas mentioned, and try to see what would make it so attractive to live there.

Finally, zoom in on the east bank of the Jordan, just across from Jericho. Show where the Israelites crossed the Jordan, to get into the Promised Land. Read Deuteronomy 8:7–10 to discover why the land God was giving them would be so good.

Living Scripture

You will need: copies of the resource sheet 'Judges Consequences' on page 32 or downloaded from www.scriptureunion.org.uk/msbible; Bibles; pens.

Set the scene in this way:

The story since last time: God rescued his people from slavery in Egypt and led them into the desert towards the land he had promised them long ago. God's covenant with them gave them absolute certainty about his faithfulness to them as their God, and as his people they needed to obey him faithfully in return. All the laws – including the Ten Commandments – showed them what that would mean.

But they moaned and groaned their way through the desert, saying how much they'd rather be back in Egypt, and eventually refusing to go into the Promised Land. So the generation that had come out of Egypt died on the journey, leaving their children to cross the Jordan into Canaan under the leadership of Joshua. God's judgement and saving grace go hand in hand.

Divide the group in two. It doesn't matter if there are only one or two in each 'group'. Give one group the Bible passage Judges 2:10–23 to explore, and the other Judges 10:6–16 and 11:29–32. Using copies of the resource sheet, they should try to fill in the blanks in the cycle as fully as possible. To start off, one person from each group should read the verses aloud to the rest.

When both groups have finished, get them to share their discoveries.

Finally, read Joshua 21:43–45, which summarises the point we have reached in the history of God's people. In what way does the statement sum up the past judges period, and in what way does it look forward to the future?

 Touching God

Scenes of life
You will need: ambient music; labels; the pictures downloaded from www.scriptureunion.org.uk/msbible and printed to A4 size.

The repeated cycle of events in the book of Judges – faithlessness, disaster, despair, pleading and rescue – mirrors what often happens in our own lives with God. We drift away, we struggle, we cry out to him, he meets us and draws us back. Play the music and allow everyone to reflect on this cycle in their own lives and to respond to God about it, using the following pictures to help them. They can pick them up and put them down at any time in any order. Label each item:

> 'faithlessness': someone wandering off the path
> 'disaster': car crash
> 'despair': tears
> 'pleading': someone knocking on a door
> 'rescue': mountain rescue team with someone who has been lost

Camcorder memories

You will need: a phone video camera or flip cam.

Encourage everyone to think of one thing they believe God has taught them this session. Then pass the flip cam or phone round the group without turning it off between contributions. Everyone briefly records their thoughts. Make it fun. If someone dramatically messes up, have a laugh and start the whole round over again!

Afterwards, whoever owns the flip cam or phone can upload the results to the group's Facebook page.

Reaching out

The book of Judges is all about God's people heading into unknown territory. Well, not exactly 'unknown', but why not hold your next session in a local coffee shop or eating place? Maybe group members could invite a friend to join you for some or all of the session. Make it clear that you're going to be talking about God so there are no surprises when people turn up! The session is written in such a way as to make it possible to do it huddled round a table somewhere, rather than in a larger space.

Digging deeper

Multi-Sensory Bible journals with a difference

You will need: copies of the resource sheet on page 10 or downloaded from www.scriptureunion. org.uk/msbible.

If the Multi-Sensory Bible journals are working well, encourage everyone to keep going with them. For their theme exploration, get them to make a note of the Bible passages at the top of page 29.

When they have done this, invite them to show what they have written to another Christian, someone who has time to listen. This person could then pray that the group member will grow more and more confident in their life with God during the Multi-Sensory Bible sessions, and learn to play their full part in the epic of God's salvation plan.

More judges

The book of Judges tells of the time between the crossing of the River Jordan and the arrival on the scene of Judge Samuel, a prophet. During those 170 or so years (roughly 1220 to 1050 BC), many judges became saviours of Israel, but God didn't choose them because they were perfect – far from it.

Give everyone another judge to study about whom we know more, so they'll be able to report briefly next time on the good and not-so-good aspects of their life:

> Deborah and Barak: Judges 4,5
> Gideon: 6:11 – 8:35
> Samson: 13:1 – 16:31

Judges Consequences

1. The Israelites . . . . 2. Their enemies . . . . 3. Finally the Israelites . . . . 4. God . . . . 5. The result was that . . . .

7 They did it their way
Kings and queen of Judah and Israel

1 Samuel 13:1–15; 15:1–11; 31:1–13; 2 Samuel 5:1–10; 7:1–16; 11:1–17; 1 Kings 3:1–15; 5:1–7; 11:1–13,41–43; 1 Chronicles 29:10–20

During the time of the judges, Israel wasn't a united people with a consistent, national approach to defeating their enemies. This judge worked in that part of the nation when enemy X threatened them; that judge fought somewhere else when enemy Y caused trouble. It was all very disjointed, but of course part of God's big plan.

The last judge was Samuel. He wasn't a soldier judge like the others, but a prophet, against the threat of the Philistines. At this point the Israelites wanted a warrior king like other people around them. Samuel advised against having one – it would indicate a lack of trust in God as the one true saviour because the kind of king God was looking for is described in Deuteronomy 17:14–20.

Saul was chosen as king, then David and Solomon. There followed a long line of kings, and a queen, Athaliah. When the nation split in two, some ruled over Judah in the south and some over Israel in the north. Each one either did or didn't do things God's way.

This session will undoubtedly cover a lot of new ground for your group. Pray that they'll really connect with the history, because they see God at work in and through it.

 Getting connected

More journals, more judges
Invite everyone to share their journal findings from last time. Are there any connections between what people are discovering? What might God be saying to you as a group about the part you're playing in the epic story of salvation that he's working out?

Also talk about some of the good and not-so-good aspects of the judges' lives that everyone looked for. Draw out from this that God chooses and uses us, not because we're perfect, but because we say 'Yes' to him as Lord of our lives and are willing to be obedient. To what extent does this resonate with anyone's experience?

OR

King or queen for a day
You will need: a cardboard or toy golden crown (optional).

With refreshments at the start of the session, ask group members, if they were king or queen for a day, what they would change and why – not a royal with restricted powers like the English monarch, but completely free. Even more, from that day onwards any changes they made would be permanent.

As each person describes what they would do, get them to wear the crown. (If you're in the coffee shop as suggested last time, you may want to leave the crown!)

Living Scripture

You will need: copies of the resource sheet 'Kings and queen' (page 36) or downloaded from www.scriptureunion.org.uk/msbible; Bibles; pens.

Use the timeline on page 37 to locate the period in history, attaching it to Part 1 (page 23). Then examine the lives of Saul, David and Solomon, Israel's first three kings. Explore the beginning, the middle and end of their reigns, to get the gist of what happened.

	Beginning	Middle	End
Saul	1 Samuel 13:1–15	1 Samuel 15:1–11	1 Samuel 31:1–13
David	2 Samuel 5:1–10	2 Samuel 7:1–16; 11:1–17	1 Chronicles 29:10–20
Solomon	1 Kings 3:1–15	1 Kings 5:1–7	1 Kings 11:1–13, 41–43

What was good about the reigns of all three kings?

Where can we catch glimpses of the kind of king Jesus will be?

It will probably be best if you split the group into three smaller teams to explore the passages around each of the three kings and answer these two (not-so-easy) questions. One or two people in a team will be fine.

Encourage everyone to feed back briefly, but sticking closely to the two questions.

Now set up the rest of the kings' story in this way:

After Solomon died, the nation split apart. The tribes of Judah and Benjamin (and probably part of Simeon) in the south stayed faithful to Solomon's son Rehoboam. The other tribes wanted Jeroboam as king. The nation divided – the southern part was called Judah, and the northern part Israel. From then on there was a mix of rulers who either did things God's way, or didn't.

Ask everyone to get into pairs or threes for the next few minutes. Distribute copies of the resource sheet to each grouping. Challenge them to find out from the Bible verses whether each king or queen mostly obeyed, or disobeyed, God. Occasionally there may be some 'Don't knows'. Make it a race for an extra bit of fun. The losers can buy the next round of coffee!

Ask the group for a response to what they have discovered. To what extent did their findings surprise them? The good news is that God never gave up on his people but promised that one day they would have the best king ever (Isaiah 9:6,7).

Touching God

Only you

You will need: the song *'Only you'* downloaded and ready to show from www.worshiphousemedia. com (you will need to pay); blank sheets of card and a variety of art and craft media, such as tissue paper, glue sticks, sticky stars etc.

Many of the kings of Israel and Judah were drawn away from worshipping the One True God by the lure of the foreign gods of peoples around them. The song video *'Only you'* is all about keeping God Number One in our lives. Watch it with the group in an attitude of prayer.

Then encourage group members to take a sheet of card and use the art and craft materials to create a visual image that helps them express their faith and love.

Jesus the King

You will need: as many different translations of the Bible as possible.

Get the group to read aloud Matthew 12:29, in as many Bible versions as possible. Explain that this is a picture of Jesus the King, invading the territory of Satan, by healing demon-possessed people and liberating them. Discuss how this demonstrates what kind of king Jesus is.

 Reaching out

Ask if anyone in the group fancies becoming a blogger for the group. After each session they could blog about anything that particularly struck them that the group discovered. The key thing with blogging is that the person has to be committed – not just writing it a couple of times, but all the time the group is doing Multi-Sensory Bible.

 Digging deeper

Multi-Sensory Bible journals

You will need: copies of the resource sheet on page 10 or downloaded from www.scriptureunion. org.uk/msbible.

Distribute the copies of the journal sheet as usual, and ask everyone to note the Bible references that are at the top of page 33. The group might also benefit from looking at the whole life of just one of Israel's first three kings. Easy – they just take the 'beginning' reference and keep on reading until they reach the 'end' one! Remind them which references relate to which king.

Movie quotes

'Seize the day! Make your lives extraordinary' (Mr Keating, played by Robin Williams in *Dead Poets' Society*, 1989, Touchstone Pictures, directed by Peter Weir and written by Tom Schulman).

Challenge your group to come up with more movie quotes that reflect something of the period of the kings and queen of Judah and Israel.

KINGS AND QUEEN

	Mostly obeyed God	Mostly disobeyed God	Don't know
KINGS OF JUDAH			
Rehoboam: 931 BC; *2 Chronicles 12:13,14*			
Abijah: 913–911 BC; *1 Kings 15:1–3*			
Asa: 911–870 BC; *1 Kings 15:9–11*			
Jehoshaphat: 870–848 BC; *1 Kings 22:41–43*			
Jehoram: 848–841 BC; *2 Kings 8:16–19*			
Ahaziah: 841 BC; *2 Kings 8:25–27*			
Joash: 835–796 BC; *2 Kings 12:1–3*			
Amaziah: 796–767 BC; *2 Kings 14:1–4*			
Azariah (also called Uzziah): 767–740 BC; *2 Kings 15:1–3*			
Jotham: 740–732 BC; *2 Kings 15:32–34*			
Ahaz: 732–716 BC; *2 Kings 16:1,2*			
Hezekiah: 716–687 BC; *2 Kings 18:1–3*			
Manasseh: 687–643 BC; *2 Kings 21:1,2*			
Amon: 643–641 BC; *2 Kings 21:19–22*			
Josiah: 640–609 BC; *2 Kings 22:1,2*			
Jehoahaz: 609 BC; *2 Kings 23:31,32*			
Jehoiakim: 609–597 BC; *2 Kings 23:35–37*			
Jehoiachin: 597 BC; *2 Kings 24:8,9*			
Zedekiah: 597–587 BC; *2 Kings 24:18–20*			
QUEEN OF JUDAH			
Athaliah: 841–835 BC; *2 Chronicles 24:7*			
KINGS OF ISRAEL			
Jeroboam I: 931–910 BC; *1 Kings 13:33,34*			
Nadab: 910–909 BC; *1 Kings 15:25,26*			
Baasha: 909–886 BC; *1 Kings 15:33,34*			
Elah: 886–885 BC; *1 Kings 16:12,13*			
Zimri: 885 BC; *1 Kings 16:17–19*			
Tibni: 885–880 BC; *1 Kings 16:21,22*			
Omri: 880–874 BC; *1 Kings 16:12,13*			
Ahab: 874–853 BC; *1 Kings 16:30,31*			
Ahaziah: 853–852 BC; *2 Kings 1:15,16*			
Jehoram: 852–841 BC; *2 Kings 3:1–3*			
Jehu: 841–814 BC; *2 Kings 10:28–31*			
Jehoahaz: 814–798 BC; *2 Kings 13:1,2*			
Jehoash: 798–782 BC; *2 Kings 13:11*			
Jeroboam II: 782–753 BC; *2 Kings 14:23,24*			
Zechariah: 753–752 BC; *2 Kings 15:8,9*			
Shallum: 752 BC; *2 Kings 15:13*			
Menahem: 752–742 BC; *2 Kings 15:17,18*			
Pekahiah: 742–740 BC; *2 Kings 15:23,24*			
Pekah: 740–732 BC; *2 Kings 15:27,28*			
Hoshea: 732–723 BC; *2 Kings 17:1,2*			

Bible timeline Part 2

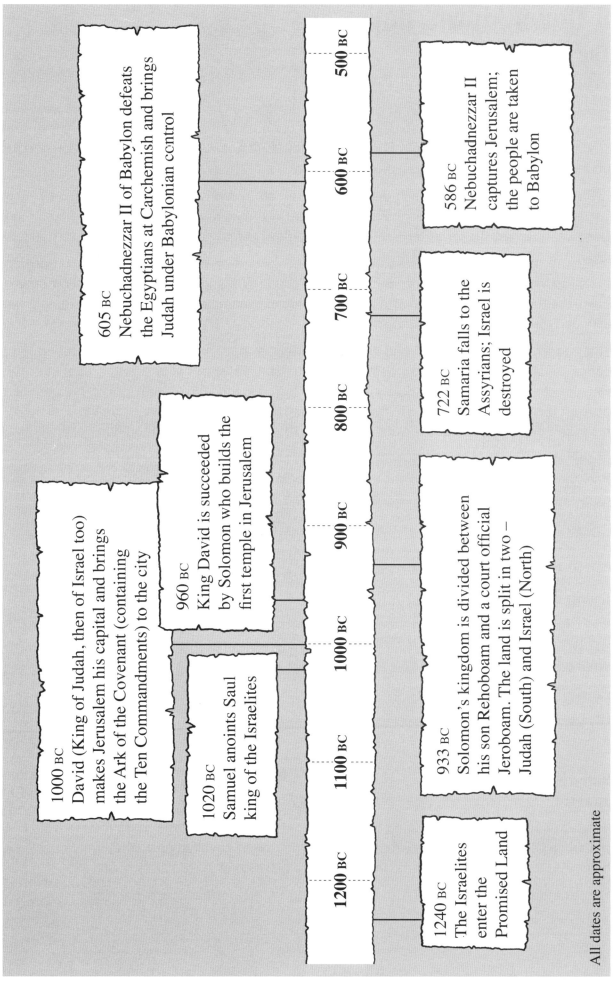

1240 BC
The Israelites enter the Promised Land

1020 BC
Samuel anoints Saul king of the Israelites

1000 BC
David (King of Judah, then of Israel too) makes Jerusalem his capital and brings the Ark of the Covenant (containing the Ten Commandments) to the city

960 BC
King David is succeeded by Solomon who builds the first temple in Jerusalem

933 BC
Solomon's kingdom is divided between his son Rehoboam and a court official Jeroboam. The land is split in two – Judah (South) and Israel (North)

722 BC
Samaria falls to the Assyrians; Israel is destroyed

605 BC
Nebuchadnezzar II of Babylon defeats the Egyptians at Carchemish and brings Judah under Babylonian control

586 BC
Nebuchadnezzar II captures Jerusalem; the people are taken to Babylon

1200 BC   1100 BC   1000 BC   900 BC   800 BC   700 BC   600 BC   500 BC

All dates are approximate

8 Down, down, down, up
The exile

Isaiah 51:3, 55:6–13; 2 Kings 25:8–21; Psalm 137

The kings and queen of Judah and Israel mostly disobeyed God, and their people followed suit. Prophets warned them of the looming, dire consequences of their rebellion, but they never took any notice, at least not for long. Consequently, in 722 BC, the Assyrians destroyed Israel (to the north), and the nation never recovered.

Even this wasn't enough to teach the people of Judah (to the south) a lesson, as Ezekiel saw. The story of the two prostitutes in Ezekiel 23:1–13 is a particularly graphic warning from God! Dead set on going their own ways rather than God's, the Judaeans headed for destruction too.

In 597 BC, the Babylonians seized Jerusalem and carried off many of its citizens to Babylon. Zedekiah was made king, under Babylonian direction and control. When he rebelled against them, the Babylonians were quick to wipe out Jerusalem completely, in 586 BC. The Temple was flattened, the people exiled to Babylon.

The tragedy about which God had warned his people, bent on sin and rebellion for so long, came about. God's judgement was clear, but as usual so were his love and grace. Into exile with the people of Judah went Ezekiel and Daniel; even in the face of what looked like complete disaster for the plans of God – with his people now hundreds of miles away from the land he had promised them – God made it clear that he would restore them, their land, their city and their temple (Ezekiel 36:33–38). Sin wouldn't have the final word.

Pray that through this session your group will begin to explore honestly where they stand with God – doubting and distant, or confident and close.

 Getting connected

Living a long way away
As you have refreshments, find out from your group members if anyone has experienced living a long way away from what they would call 'home'.

What did they need to adjust to?

How long did it take to adjust?

Did they ever feel as if the other place were 'home'?

OR

Video journals
You will need: a mobile video camera or flip cam.

Instead of everyone simply sharing their journal findings from last time, pass around a flip cam or mobile and record everyone's responses. Ask the same question as before: What might God be saying to you as a group about the part you're playing in the epic story of salvation?

One of the group could edit the video and upload it to your Facebook page or the blog that someone may have started since last time.

Living Scripture

You will need: Bibles; the signs 'Jerusalem', 'Babylon this way' and 'Isaiah's place' downloaded from www.scriptureunion.org.uk/msbible and printed on card.

Display the sign 'Jerusalem' in one corner of your room, as far from the door as possible, and 'Babylon this way' pointing out of the door. Also put 'Isaiah's place' on a chair just outside 'Jerusalem'. In advance, choose someone to be Isaiah and to sit on the labelled chair, ready to read Isaiah 51:3 and 55:6–13.

As you all (apart from 'Isaiah') gather in 'Jerusalem', set the scene in this way:

The story since last time: In the northern kingdom of Israel and the southern kingdom of Judah, God's people and their kings and queen were lying, cheating and worshipping other gods. You could hardly tell the difference between them and all the pagan tribes around them! But God loved them so much that he sent prophets to warn them. Hosea and Amos told the people of Israel that the Assyrians would wipe them out if they didn't get back to living God's way. The people of Israel ignored them and, sure enough, the Assyrians carted them off to Assyria as prisoners. They never came back. That was the end of Israel! But Judah escaped … for the time being!

Get 'Isaiah' to kick off the story by reading his verses, from Isaiah 51 and 55. 'Isaiah' can stay where he is.

Now read 2 Kings 25:8–21 together. Pause when you reach the end of verse 10, get someone to tear up the 'Jerusalem' sign and throw the pieces in the air. Say that this took place in 597 BC, then carry on reading.

When you reach the end of verse 11, send half the group into 'exile' just outside the door, but with the door open so that they can hear what's going on. Ask them to be ready to read Psalm 137 aloud all together when you have finished reading the 2 Kings verses. Now read on from verse 12.

At the end of verse 21, the 'exiles' read out Psalm 137.

When you have finished, gather everyone back together and discuss these questions:

With regard to God's covenant promises in Genesis (see page 18), why does the exile seem so disastrous?

This is certainly a time of judgement for God's people, but where do we see God still loving and promising?

 Touching God

Songs in a foreign land

You will need: the song books your church uses, or a laptop with song words on it.

'Sing us one of the songs of Zion', taunted the captors of God's people (Psalm 137:3). Today we might say, though not in a taunting way, 'Sing us one of those Christian songs you find helpful when you're down.' Ask for volunteers to share a suggestion and why they chose it, then sing one or two.

Budding and flourishing

You will need: a small, budding plant for each group member; a Bible.

The bud represents what you long for in the life of each group member – new life and growth brought about by God's Word. Read aloud Isaiah 55:10,11, then give two or three group members a plant each, adding the words 'In your life, (name of the person)' as you give it to them. Now say the Bible verses again and address two or three more people. Repeat the process until all the plants have been distributed and all group members prayed for.

Encourage everyone to look after their plant. Each time they tend to it, they can pray for God's Word to be at work in their life.

 Reaching out

Think of those who used to come to your church and were once excited about being God's people, and then cooled off and left. What could you do to connect with them again? It may be easier for them to re-connect with just one or two group members rather than walk into church again.

 Digging deeper

Prophets still speaking

You will need: a copy of the resource sheet on page 41 for each person or downloaded and printed in colour from www.scriptureunion.org.uk/msbible; Bibles; pens.

When Old Testament prophets spoke, they often had one or more of these messages from God for his people:
The people had broken their covenant promises to God and had sinned against him;
God would judge them; But one day he would restore them.

Distribute copies of the sheet, for group members to work through individually and in their own time. Encourage them to let God speak to them through the words of the prophets. Group members could do this instead of the usual journal activity.

The Bible in 50 words

You will need: small prizes; copies of the resource sheet on page 19 or downloaded from www.scriptureunion.org.uk/msbible.

Recap on the lines already learnt by heart. Challenge everyone to say them together without looking at the sheet. Now learn up to the end of line 16, 'Prophets warned'. Offer a small prize to anyone who can now say it on their own!

Prophets still speaking

Read the sets of verses and reflect on each image. Then read your own life, see the similarities with the verses and the image, and write a prayer of response to God.

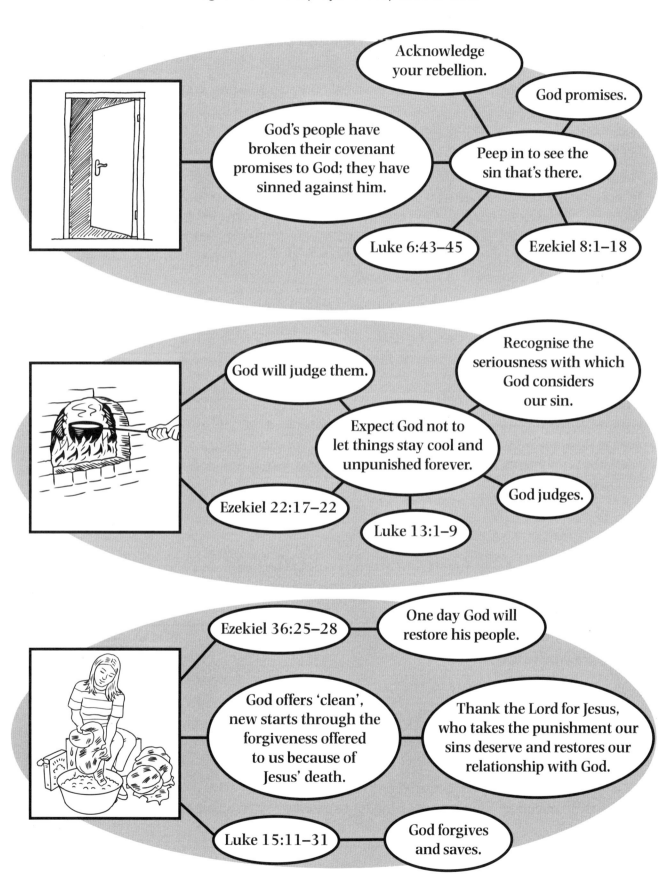

Acknowledge your rebellion.

God promises.

God's people have broken their covenant promises to God; they have sinned against him.

Peep in to see the sin that's there.

Luke 6:43–45

Ezekiel 8:1–18

God will judge them.

Recognise the seriousness with which God considers our sin.

Expect God not to let things stay cool and unpunished forever.

Ezekiel 22:17–22

God judges.

Luke 13:1–9

Ezekiel 36:25–28

One day God will restore his people.

God offers 'clean', new starts through the forgiveness offered to us because of Jesus' death.

Thank the Lord for Jesus, who takes the punishment our sins deserve and restores our relationship with God.

Luke 15:11–31

God forgives and saves.

9 Not exactly home and dry
The Jews return from exile

Ezra 1:1–6; 3:8–13; Haggai 1:3–15; 2:6–9; Malachi 4:1–6

You'd think that nothing could have been better for the Jews than to hear that they could return to their 'promised land' and rebuild their temple. It was certainly good news for them, but it turned out not to be the great moment of salvation that their prophets had predicted. They would be home, but not exactly home and dry.

The Jews returned home not because their nation had somehow come out strongest in the Middle-Eastern power struggle, but because Medo-Persian King Cyrus had conquered the Babylonians. Their new captor simply happened to look more kindly on them and sent them back home.

There, Jerusalem and the Temple were in ruins. God had chosen the city to represent his name. To outsiders, a ruin of a city would suggest a ruin of a God. Also, a city without walls would make the people vulnerable, belying one possible meaning of the city's name. 'Yeruslem' (with echoes of the Hebrew word for 'peace' or 'wholeness' – 'shalom') suggested a 'city of peace' and security. The city and Temple just had to be rebuilt, and the Jews had to survive for God's long-term plan to work out.

Pray that through these sessions, your group members will come to know true peace.

 Getting connected

God having spoken...
Over refreshments, ask if anyone heard from God as they either did the 'Prophets still speaking' activity, or went with the usual 'Multi-Sensory Bible journals' time. Help them to look for and value these moments as times when God is growing faith in them. A sense of expectation is important.

OR

Waiting
You will need: slips of paper and pens.

Tell each other stories of times when you found it hard to wait for something good to happen. It might have been a birthday or Christmas treat, the birth of a child or the most amazing holiday imaginable. Or perhaps it was something special you longed for God to do.

What were you waiting for?

Why were you looking forward to it so much?

When the time actually came, did it meet your expectations?

Distribute paper and a pen to each group member. Ask them to draw on separate slips what they think God's people in exile might have been looking forward to.

When everyone has finished, get everyone to lay their slips out in the middle of the group. They should try to match up what they have thought about with what others have drawn.

Can the group see any themes emerging?

Living Scripture

You will need: the drawings the group made in 'Waiting', if you did this activity; the four cards cut out from resource page 45; a gold or silver bowl; some water in an earthenware bowl; a small piece of carved wood; a candle and matches; Bibles.

Set the scene like this:

The story since last time: The Jews were in exile in Babylon for around 70 years. (If you did the activity, invite group members to recount what they drew on their slips in 'Waiting'.) God's people have long since heard prophecies of a great return from exile to their homeland. However, this happens not because they have become the number one nation, but because in 538 BC the Persians take over Babylon, Cyrus the Persian king shows them kindness and lets them return to re-establish their nation. So is this the moment for the long-promised kingdom of God to be set up, with God's best king seated on the throne?

Encourage everyone to listen very carefully to the descriptions of the events of the return from exile. Distribute the four cards to group members who will be happy to read out the Bible verses printed on them. Everyone else can follow in their own Bible.

As each person reads their verses in turn, place the appropriate object (as illustrated on the card) in the centre of the group. As each person finishes reading their verses, they place the card near the object.

Now remove the four cards, leaving only the objects. Use the objects as prompts and work together to retell the story with the kind of phrases used in the Bible verses. Connect your retelling to the themes of: God creates; God provides; God shapes and leads; God forgives; God saves/rescues; God judges; God promises; God reveals who he is.

 Touching God

The hopes and fears of all the years
You will need: the pot of water you used for 'Living Scripture'; a teaspoon; a towel.

Like the Jews returning from exile, and the disciples Jesus was leaving behind (John 14:27), we too live in hurting, imperfect, fearful times; we long to be 'at home', 'safe', 'at peace'.

Place a teaspoon of water into the palm of each group member's hand. In their own time, each person tips a drop of water from one hand onto the other. Each drop represents a tear and a particular fear. With each drop, they pray silently that God will take away their fear and replace it with hope.

Our timelines

You will need: the three sections of the 'Bible timeline' either downloaded from www.scriptureunion. org.uk/msbible or photocopied from pages 23, 37 and 46 to A3 size, and stuck together into one long strip; felt markers.

Stick the Bible timeline to a hard surface so that group members can write on it. Give everyone a felt marker. Go through the whole story, tracing the ups and downs of God's people. What made the 'ups' up, and the 'downs' down? Note a word or phrase at each peak or trough in the story.

Encourage everyone to think about then tell the story of their life with God, starting from their birth (their 'genesis') through to the present day. To what extent does it match or differ from the story of God's people?

 ## Reaching out

You will need: cards, paper, pens, party food and drink.

Now that we have reached the end of the Old Testament, celebrate with an OTT party (Old Testament Teasers)! Everyone should come dressed as an Old Testament character, keeping their identity a secret. They should write three or four clues to their identity on a card, and pin the card to the back of their costume. Hand out paper and pens, and see who can guess the most OT characters during the course of the party.

This might be an event to invite friends to, or you might think they'd do better to avoid it!

 ## Digging deeper

Multi-Sensory Bible journals

You will need: copies of the resource sheet on page 10 or downloaded from www.scriptureunion. org.uk/msbible.

Distribute the copies of the journal sheet as usual, and ask everyone to note the Bible references that are at the top of page 42. Also add Zechariah 9:9,10 as an extra reading. We're more than halfway through Multi-Sensory Bible now, so encourage everyone to keep going to the end.

Song of revival

Use Psalm 85 to stimulate prayer. First read the psalm together, and then discuss:

If this psalm were used by God's people at the time of their return from exile, what connections might they have made between the words and their experiences?

Now use the psalm to stimulate prayer about your own lives:

vs 1–3: Read, then recall God's goodness to you in the past. Thank him.

vs 4–7: Pray for forgiveness. Ask God to get you back in the right place with him.

vs 8,9: Listen to God. Enjoy the thought that God will dwell with you again, intimately, bringing peace into your life.

vs 10–13: Pray for help to move on with God and to live his way, in 'righteousness'.

Living Scripture

1

Ezra 1:1–6

2

Haggai
1:3–15; 2:6–9

3

Ezra 3:8–13

4

Malachi 4:1–6

Bible timeline Part 3

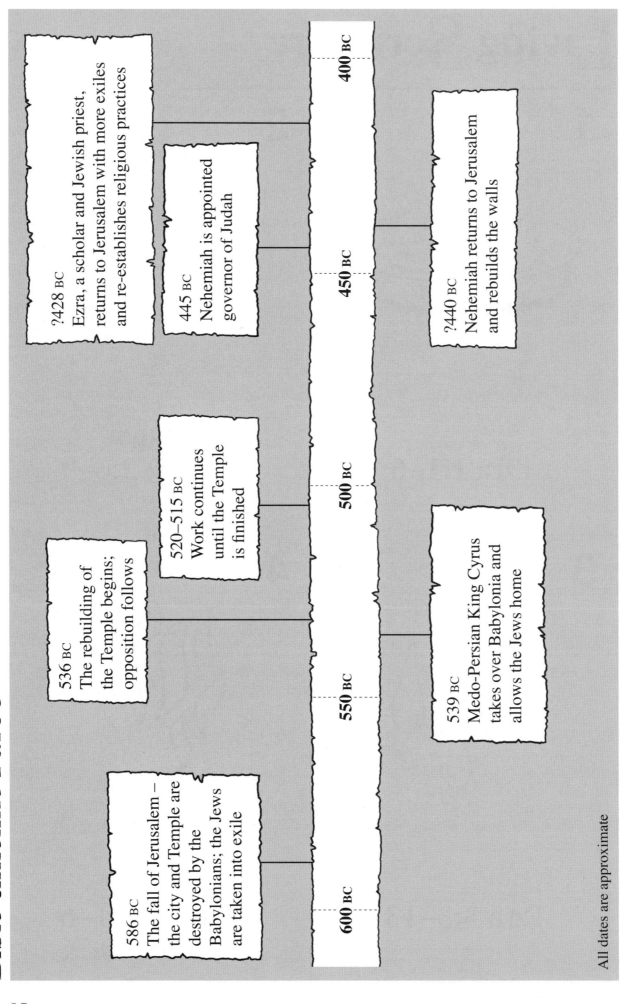

586 BC
The fall of Jerusalem – the city and Temple are destroyed by the Babylonians; the Jews are taken into exile

536 BC
The rebuilding of the Temple begins; opposition follows

520–515 BC
Work continues until the Temple is finished

?428 BC
Ezra, a scholar and Jewish priest, returns to Jerusalem with more exiles and re-establishes religious practices

445 BC
Nehemiah is appointed governor of Judah

?440 BC
Nehemiah returns to Jerusalem and rebuilds the walls

539 BC
Medo-Persian King Cyrus takes over Babylonia and allows the Jews home

600 BC

550 BC

500 BC

450 BC

400 BC

All dates are approximate

10 Promise fulfilled
The birth and ministry of Jesus

Matthew 1:1–25; Luke 7:18–35

From the creation of everything to the prompting of the post-exilic prophets Haggai, Zechariah and Malachi, one big story is being told. God saved and shaped his people: as they journeyed into Egypt as slaves and were then rescued; as they moaned their way through the desert; as God gave them rules for living and being his people; as they entered the Promised Land and constantly struggled to obey God there; as they were taken into exile and then returned for the rebuilding of Jerusalem.

And all the time, however good or bad things got, there was the promise that the experience of the saving relationship God offered would somehow be even better in the future, and freely extended to all peoples of the world.

The life, death and resurrection of Jesus, Son of God and Son of Man, are the climax of the story. Through him, all the rest makes sense and all the promises are fulfilled. 'We tell you the good news: what God promised our ancestors he has fulfilled for us, their children, by raising up Jesus' (Acts 13:32,33).

Pray that in this session all the jigsaw pieces will fall into place for your group members, as you see all the Multi-Sensory Bible themes, all the actions and nature of God, brought into focus in Jesus.

 Getting connected

Multi-Sensory Bible journals
Offer refreshments and the opportunity for group members to feed back on their discoveries. If by now they are used to connecting the themes of the Bible narratives with the story of their own life with God, they may be ready to pray for each other, for any of the issues the journaling activity has raised over the sessions.

OR

42 generations
You will need: the name cards on pages 50 to 52 downloaded from www.scriptureunion.org.uk/msbible or photocopied, and cut up; Bibles; string or a washing line; pegs.

This is a recap session on the Old Testament, leading into the New. It helps point to Jesus as the fulfilment of God's promise to Abram (Genesis 12:1–3) and of the promise that God's throne and kingdom will be established for ever (2 Samuel 7:16). Look up and read out these verses.

Shuffle the cards and distribute them randomly around the group. Get everyone to look up any Bible verses printed on their character cards (not all have a verse). Each person will be responsible for saying how the characters they are holding fit into the big story of the Old Testament, if we know.

Read Matthew 1:1–24, pausing at the end of verses 6, 11 and 16 for everyone to peg up their characters in order and to say as much about them as they can.

(NB If you noticed there are only 41 names on the cards, well spotted! For an explanation see the website.)

Living Scripture

You will need: Bibles.

Set the scene in the following way:

The story since last time: 'The long silence' it's sometimes called – it was the time between the prophets who spoke after the Exile and the coming of Jesus into the world as a baby. Plenty had happened to God's people during those 400 years, but mostly it was one kind of oppression after another – from Persians, to Greeks, to Romans. The Jews were waiting for the fulfilment of God's promises – the ultimate King, the full experience of salvation, the dwelling of God on earth, the crushing of Satan, the start of the blessings of all the nations on earth that God had promised Abram. And the fulfilment was in Jesus.

John the Baptist had baptised Jesus, but was now in prison. He was expecting Jesus to do amazing things, especially acts of judgement, but so far nothing much seemed to have happened. Read Luke 7:18–35 with different group members reading the parts of the Narrator, Jesus and two of John's disciples.

Jesus came to preach, teach and heal, but he wasn't just another preacher, teacher and healer. Discuss the following questions together:

1 Compare what Isaiah says about the Messiah (the Anointed One, God's Chosen One, the Saviour) in Isaiah 35 and 61:1–3 with what Jesus says about himself here.

2 In verse 28, Jesus is saying that John is part of the age that was waiting for the promise of the Messiah and the kingdom to be fulfilled; anyone who is part of the long-promised rule that God is bringing in through Jesus is in a far better position than John. Jesus' life is the decisive, pivotal point of the story of God, his people and his kingdom.

3 Picture two groups of children playing in the street. One taunts the other for not joining in with their fun. Why do you think Jesus uses this image to describe 'the people of this generation' (vs 31–35)?

 Touching God

Jesus' rule
You will need: ambient music; pens; paper or Multi-Sensory Bible journals.

'If Jesus is king, I am not. If Jesus is centre stage, I cannot be. If Jesus calls, I follow. How can heaven's kingdom be seen, unless in me?' (Graham Cray, *Encounter with God*, Scripture Union, 2011).

Play the music, read aloud the above quote, and invite group members to list or draw on paper or in their journal everything they value highly. Then encourage them to pray that Jesus will take the highest place, and God's kingdom will grow in them.

Such love

Read aloud the following retold version of Mark 1:40–45. Ask everyone to close their eyes and imagine themselves as the man with leprosy – damaged nerves, twisted hands, lumps on the face, flattened nose, partial blindness, and bandaged, hurting feet. A miserable existence.

The man with leprosy came close to Jesus. 'Hey, you!' the crowd shouted. 'You can't do that!' But the man did it. Then Jesus touched the man everyone else kept away from, afraid. 'Hey, you!' they shouted at Jesus. 'You can't do that!' Yes, Jesus could, and he did! And straightaway, the man's leprosy disappeared.

Now the man could be with his family and friends again, where he had longed to be. He could do a job and earn his livelihood. He could live again! Jesus gave him back his whole life.

So amazing was God's power, working through Jesus. So strong was God's love, shown by Jesus. Jesus is God, and God rules.

Ask your group members how it made them want to respond to Jesus.

 Reaching out

Jesus' ministry was to preach, teach and heal – bold words of truth and life-changing acts of compassion. Plan together how you can reach out to your local community with the good news and love of Jesus, but in an original and creative way. How can you bring 'healing' as well as an understanding and experience of who Jesus is and what he came to do?

 Digging deeper

Listen to Mark

Invite group members to listen to an audio recording of the whole Gospel of Mark. It will take about 90 minutes, but will make far more impact if they hear it all in one sitting. There's a great, free download of it called *You've Got the Time*, in three podcast episodes at www.biblesociety. org.uk/support-us/ygtt-2010/.

Hold in mind the Multi-Sensory Bible themes as you listen, to see how all that took place in the Old Testament was fulfilled in Jesus.

Multi-Sensory Bible journals

You will need: copies of the resource sheet on page 10 or downloaded from www.scriptureunion. org.uk/msbible.

Distribute the sheet as usual, and ask everyone to note the Bible references that are at the top of page 47.

As part of your group members' time of 'digging deeper', encourage them to draw their own family tree, as far back as they can go, and trace the work of God through it. It might help them to go to ancestry.co.uk or a similar research site. Perhaps next time they could share their discoveries with the group.

42 Generations

Abraham
Genesis 12:1–3

Isaac
Genesis 17:19

Jacob
Genesis 28:12–15

Judah
Genesis 49:1,2,8;   Ruth 4:12

Perez (and Zerah)
Ruth 4:18–22

Hezron
Ruth 4:18–22

Ram
Ruth 4:18–22

Amminadab
1 Chronicles 15:4,10;   Ruth 4:18–22

Nahshon
Exodus 6:23   Numbers 2:3,4   Numbers 10:14

Salmon
Ruth 4:18–22

Boaz
Ruth 4:9,10

Obed
Ruth 4:13,16,17

Jesse
1 Samuel 16:10,11

King David
1 Samuel 16:1,13

42 Generations

Solomon
1 Kings 4:29–34

Rehoboam
1 Kings 11:42,43

Abijah
2 Chronicles 13:1,2

Asa
2 Chronicles 16:1,2

Jehoshaphat
2 Chronicles 17:1–6

Jehoram
2 Kings 8:16–19

Uzziah
2 Chronicles 26:1–5

Jotham
2 Chronicles 27:6

Ahaz
2 Chronicles 28:1,2,5

Hezekiah
2 Kings 18:5–7

Manasseh
2 Kings 21:1–6

Amon
2 Kings 21:19–22

Josiah
2 Kings 23:24,25

Jehoiachin (or Jeconiah)
2 Chronicles 36:9

42 Generations

Shealtiel
1 Chronicles 3:17; 2 Chronicles 36:9,10

Zerubbabel
Ezra 2:1,2   Ezra 3:1–3

Abihud

Eliakim (Two possibilities)
Nehemiah 12:38–41   Isaiah 22:19–23

Azor

Zadok

Akim

Elihud

Eleazar

Matthan

Jacob

Joseph

Jesus Christ

11 Moment of victory
Jesus' death and resurrection

Matthew 27:27–66; 28:1–20; Philippians 2:1–11

Jesus Christ comes from Abraham's family, traced through Old Testament history (Matthew 1:1–17). However, whereas God's people – Jesus' human family, Israel – constantly failed in obeying God and staying close to him, Jesus the new, true Israel, succeeded.

The covenants God made with his people in the Old Testament (for instance, with Noah in Genesis 9:8–17 and Abraham in Genesis 17:3–8, with Moses in Exodus 24 and with David in 2 Samuel 7:1–16) would be written on people's hearts (Jeremiah 31:31–34) so that there would be no 'gap' between them and God, between their will and his. In Jesus – God and man together – the covenant was perfectly fulfilled (as described in Mary's song, Luke 1:46–55), and through Jesus' death, he offered everyone in the world the closest possible relationship with God himself, their sins forgiven. Now forgiven people everywhere – Jew and Gentile – are the new people of God.

This is a vital moment in the Multi-Sensory Bible sessions. Pray that your group members will see Jesus as the fulfilment of all the hope that has been expressed in the Old Testament, and the only One who can give hope for the future.

 Getting connected

God in our family trees

Over refreshments, ask if anyone managed to trace any of their family tree since last time. Encourage them to share what they discovered of the work of God in their history. For instance, who first introduced them to the Lord Jesus? Chat about how they see God at work currently in their daily lives, and about how they would like to be remembered by future generations.

OR

Warmth of our love

You will need: the dot picture downloaded from www.scriptureunion.org.uk/msbible and printed in colour for each group member; pens.

Note: This activity may not be suitable if you have group members who are colour-blind.

Give each person a copy of the dot picture and a pen. This is a personal exercise, so they may want to keep their picture hidden from everyone else. Invite everyone to write above or below the appropriate dots, to describe when their love for Jesus has grown colder, then warmer, and so on, with a marker on the picture to show how they would describe their love right now. They may then wish to pray about what they have written.

Then lead a prayer that during this session the love of all of you for Jesus will grow warmer, as you hear about all he gave for us.

Living Scripture

Read together Matthew 27:32–66 and 28:1–20. These are long passages, to get the full story, so ask two or three group members to read them aloud rather than reading them a verse at a time.

Then discuss the following questions:

What suggestions are there in these verses that this is a king who is suffering?

What in these events seems incongruous for a king?

And what seem like the actions of the best king there could ever be?

So how would you describe the kind of king Jesus is?

Why do you think there is so much irony used in Matthew 27:32–66?

A group leader was talking about how Jesus died on the cross to some children who had never heard the story before. One little girl's eyes filled with tears. 'You mean they killed Jesus?' she said incredulously. When the leader explained that the good news was that God brought Jesus back to life again, one little boy exclaimed, 'Oh, that was lucky!' Indeed it was!

 Touching God

Jesus through objects

You will need: a pair of sandals; a few small stones; two small fish; a rustic loaf of bead; a candle; matches; a bowl of water; a towel; a piece of purple cloth; some thorns twisted roughly together into a 'crown'; a small wooden cross; a larger stone; a Bible.

Spread out the objects before everyone in the following order as you read out each Bible verse. They will help everyone focus on who Jesus is and what he has done:

1   sandals (Matthew 3:11)
2   stones (Luke 4:3)
3   two small fish (John 6:9)
4   a rustic loaf (John 6:35)
5   a candle that is safely alight (John 8:12)
6   a bowl of water and towel (John 13:4)
7   a purple cloth (Mark 15:17)
8   a crown of thorns (Matthew 27:29)
9   a cross (Acts 2:23)
10   a stone (John 20:1)

Pause for silent or spoken praise of Jesus. Then encourage group members to pick up any of the items, to use them to pray about the reality of Jesus in their own lives. God was born and lived on earth as Jesus, and died so that people like us can be forgiven of our sins simply by having faith, restored in our relationship with God, and taken to heaven.

Then read the poem 'There was no' by Stewart Henderson from *The Lion Christian Poetry Collection*, © 1995 Mary Batchelor. It's on the resource sheet on page 57.

The miracle he didn't want to perform

You will need: a copy of the resource sheet on page 56 or downloaded from www.scriptureunion. org.uk/msbible; pens; slips of coloured paper; small nails; a hammer; a wooden cross made of two rough pieces of wood nailed together; ambient music.

Read out 'The miracle he didn't want to perform' slowly, pausing as marked to allow everyone to reflect. Then give each person a pen and slip of paper. Invite them to write their personal response to what Jesus did on the cross. What do they want to say to him about it? What is written should be kept secret. Get everyone to fold their slip in half. As ambient music plays, they should come forward one at a time, pick up the hammer and a small nail, and nail their message to the cross. At the same time, they can speak their words to Jesus silently in prayer, if they want to.

 ## Reaching out

Watch a video of the life, death and resurrection of Jesus. Make it a relaxed occasion, perhaps inviting some non-Christian or fringe friends, and eating a takeaway together. The BBC drama *The Passion* (starring Joseph Mawle as Jesus) is an especially moving interpretation of the last few days of Jesus' life and ministry on earth, though there are places where it diverges significantly from the Bible text. Its running time is 180 minutes, so you may wish to split up your watching with a walk or other activity. Alternatively, choose the version you find most compelling.

 ## Digging deeper

The lamb offered up

Explore the sacrifice of Jesus, the Passover lamb, on the cross. Through death, Jesus was not only the conquering King, but also the pure Lamb of the sacrifice. Look for as many connections as you can between the way the Passover lamb is described in the Old Testament, and the way Jesus died, and what it meant:

> Genesis 22:8
> Exodus 12:1–11
> Numbers 9:9–13
> Isaiah 53
> John 1:29,36; 19:36
> Revelation 5:1–14

Multi-Sensory Bible journals

You will need: copies of the resource sheet on page 10 or downloaded from www.scriptureunion. org.uk/msbible.

Distribute the copies of the journal sheet as usual, and ask everyone to note all the Bible references that are at the top of page 53. One or two of your group may wish to get together for refreshments between sessions, to compare the discoveries they have made through their reflection in their journal. Maybe this could become a regular feature as you strengthen fellowship in the group.

The miracle he didn't want to perform

To undo three nails would have been a mere trifle for a carpenter's son. In Joseph's workshop he had worked on wood up to the age of thirty, and there he still was, stuck between wood and nails. He could tell from the smell and texture whether this wood was beech, oak or chestnut. Three nails deeply wedged into the wood's white fibre – how many he had put in and pulled out! He knew how to do it. It would have been an easy miracle, scarcely a miracle at all.

The rabble shouted: *'Come down, impostor'*; from up above he could see their mouths opening in blasphemies, their teeth gleaming in mockery and laughter. He could see the bronzed muscle-work of their shoulders, and the anxious heads of the soldiers bent over their dice. He could see his mother like a little black ant who, that evening, would remain alone on the pavements of the world...

Artist: Helen Jones

It would be a simple and quiet miracle. He would come down as from a ladder. The angels would immediately change the red holes of his wounds into roses and he would reach the ground unharmed. Having reached the ground he would go down the hill. They would go to Lazarus's house in Bethany. That very evening, in the gentle light of the two sisters, Mary would hear him telling wonderful things.

Yes, this was certainly the most necessary miracle if he wanted the world to believe in him. Get down. Nothing else would be needed, and thousands of martyrs would be spared...

We would certainly have come down. Our mothers and our common sense would have torn us down with the nails still fixed in our hands and feet. We would have run away, trailing the hill with blood, towards the throne onto which terrified men who realised their mistake would finally raise us.

But he didn't want to work this miracle...

We can't understand. We'll never believe that life is bought with death and that this last breath from the breast is worth more than the gold of all the stars weighing on the night. But he who had made life and death and the stars knew it, and his parched mouth answered: *'No.'*

From Wrestling with Christ, by Luigi Santucci,
published by Fontana Books, 1974

There was no

There was no grave grave enough
to ground me
to mound me
I broke the balm then slit the shroud
wound round me
that bound me

There was no death dead enough
to dull me
to cull me
I snapped the snake and waned his war
to lull me
to null me

there was no cross cross enough
to nil me
to still me
I hung as gold that bled, and bloomed
A rose that rose and prised the tomb
away from Satan's wilful doom
There was no cross, death, grave
or room
to hold me.

Stewart Henderson, from *The Lion Christian Poetry Collection,*
© 1995 Mary Batchelor

12 Upwards and onwards
Jesus' ascension and the coming of the Holy Spirit

Luke 24:36–53; Acts 1:1–11; 2:1–13

These are pivotal moments. Luke the doctor had written his Gospel for a Roman patron called Theophilus, telling the story of Jesus' life on earth (Luke 1:1–4). We don't know much about Theophilus, though his name means 'dear to God' or 'friend of God'. Perhaps the words 'most excellent' (1:3) show that he was a Roman official. Now comes Book 2 by Luke, the Acts of the Apostles (those sent by God), which tells the story of how the Christian church began and spread. This story continues today, and Christians are part of it as they share the good news of Jesus. What Jesus began, we carry on by the power of the Holy Spirit. Jesus had bridged the gap between people, creation and God that had opened up in that first rebellion in the Garden of Eden. The drawing of them all back into unity with God was well under way (Ephesians 1:8–10).

Jesus had to ascend to heaven from earth – had to so that his friends would have no doubt at all that he had returned to heaven which they believed was 'up', beyond the sky. Strangely, Jesus' followers went back to Jerusalem 'with great joy' (Luke 24:52) – somehow he would carry on being present with them and would be back (Matthew 28:20; Acts 1:11).

The connection between what they read in the New Testament and their own lives may now become more apparent to your group members. Pray that it will. People back then heard the good news, decided to follow Jesus, and their lives were reoriented around him, his ways and his mission – the reuniting of people and God. And that's exactly our story too.

 Getting connected

Multi-Sensory Bible journals plus
Offer refreshments and encourage group members to talk together about anything they have discovered from their journaling, if they haven't already done so since you last met.

OR

The day that changed everything
Encourage everyone to chat about 'the day that changed everything'. Their stories could be light and joyful, or more serious and sadder. How about if you then ask them to speak of 'the day that God changed everything'? Perhaps pause to pray or praise God together after someone's story, where it would be appropriate.

Artistic impressions
You will need: several images from the internet depicting the Ascension such as 'Ascension of Jesus' by Dinah Roe-Kendall or 'The Ascension' by Benjamin West.

Invite group members to say what they think each of the artists was trying to express about Jesus' ascension.

Living Scripture

You will need: copies of the resource sheet on page 61, or downloaded from www.scriptureunion. org.uk/msbible, enough to cut up into cards for your group members; pens.

Lead in to the activity in this way:

The story since last time: Jesus' disciples were dispirited about his death and many were unconvinced about his resurrection. When Jesus met with his disciples on earth for the last time, he told them to wait in Jerusalem until they received power from God (Luke 24:49) and even though he was going away, to be absolutely sure that he would always be with them (Matthew 28:20). But none of them could have imagined what was to follow!

Divide into two smaller groups. As long as there are at least two in each small group, it will be fine. Each will explore one Bible passage about Jesus' ascension, and then they will compare their findings.

Distribute copies of the 'Jesus' ascension' cards and pens, and set everyone to work. They should work as groups rather than as individuals.

After 10 or 15 minutes, draw everyone together again and compare findings between the two groups.

In a way we could say that the ascension was for the sake of the disciples who believed that heaven was 'up' above their heads, so they couldn't mistake the fact that Jesus had gone to heaven and not somewhere else. By his ascension, Jesus showed that his post-resurrection appearances were over and his return to heaven would bring the presence of the Holy Spirit, which he had spoken about with his disciples. It was a piece of acted symbolism. He departed to remain with his church, in fact now more than ever. While he was on earth he was not physically able to be everywhere at the same time. But now he is in heaven he is able, in and through the Holy Spirit, to be everywhere spiritually. Also, while he was on earth he was present with the church; now he is present in the church. In other words, he departed from us to draw closer to us.

 Touching God

Ripples of the Spirit
You will need: the soundtrack downloaded from www.scriptureunion.org.uk/msbible, with equipment to play it on (**Note:** the track starts quietly and gradually gets louder; it also has sound effects on it that connect with the script); the 'Ripples of the Spirit' resource sheet on page 62.

You may need to practise reading the drama along with the music track, to get the timing right.

Israeli dancing

You will need: a CD or MP3 of the song *'King of kings and Lord of lords'*, and something to play it on; also, if possible, the Hebrew song *'Hava nagila'* and Giora Feidman's *'Humoresque "halaka" dance'*, available on iTunes.

Celebrate the coming of the Holy Spirit with some Israeli-type dancing. You won't particularly need to know what you're doing – the music will take you there. However, if you'd like to add some authenticity, check out *'Hava nagila'* on YouTube.

If you're inspired, organise an evening of Israeli dancing as a social event. There may be someone from the local Jewish community who could come to lead it for you.

Reaching out

You will need: a phone camera with internet connection.

If your group had to convey to the outside world the feeling and meaning of the time when the Holy Spirit came to the followers in Jerusalem, what photos would you take? Grab someone's phone camera and set up four or five shots.

If you're really bold, you could upload them to the Facebook group you have set up. The only thing is, the photos may look weird and people might think you're drunk! (Should fit right in with most other Facebook albums then!) Now, who could you share them with?!

Digging deeper

The King is on his throne

Your group may need extra help with understanding the significance of the ascension. If so, lead them though the following additional points.

Jesus' ascension had a purpose, or rather several purposes:

Jesus had said to his disciples, 'I am going ... to prepare a place for you' (John 14:2). And here he was going, just as he had said!

Jesus sat down in heaven beside God, a sign that his atoning work was complete and final (Hebrews 10:11–14). That's where Jesus is now.

While in heaven, Jesus prays for his people (Romans 8:34; Hebrews 7:25).

Jesus is waiting until he has subdued his enemies, and he will return as the final act of establishing the kingdom of God (1 Corinthians 15:24–26).

Multi-Sensory Bible journals

You will need: copies of the resource sheet on page 10 or downloaded from www.scriptureunion. org.uk/msbible.

As usual, distribute copies of the journal page. As well as the passages listed at the top of page 58, give everyone the following references to note on their journal sheet: Acts 2:33; 3:21; Ephesians 4:8–10; Hebrews 4:14; 9:24; 1 Peter 3:22. Reassure everyone that they only need reflect on as many passages as they have time for – there's no need for them to feel they have to wade through the lot!

Jesus' ascension

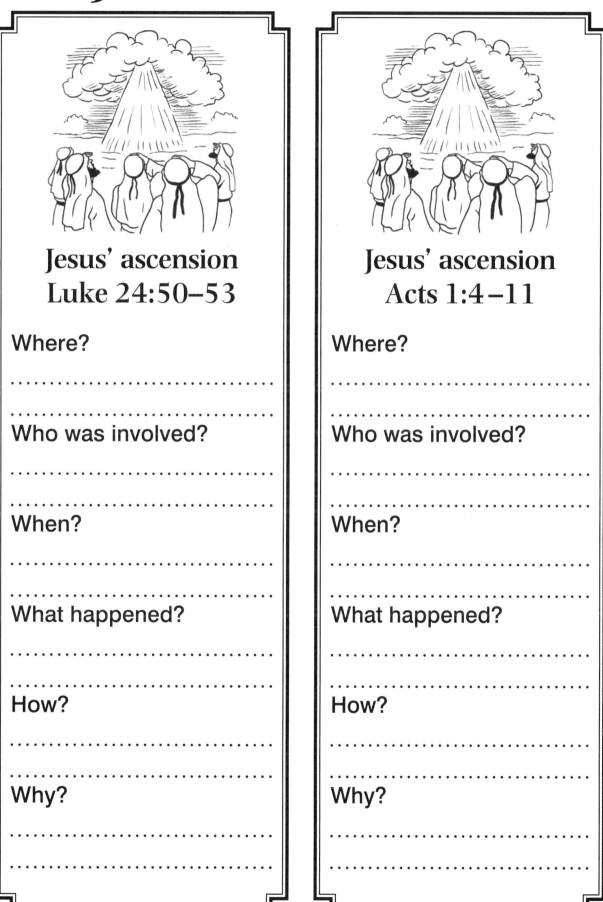

Jesus' ascension
Luke 24:50–53

Where?

....

....

Who was involved?

....

When?

....

What happened?

....

How?

....

Why?

....

....

Jesus' ascension
Acts 1:4–11

Where?

....

....

Who was involved?

....

When?

....

What happened?

....

How?

....

Why?

....

....

Ripples of the Spirit

(Put on the soundtrack.)

This is not *(say the year when you're doing this session)*.
It's about seven weeks after Jesus died and rose again from death.

And this isn't *(name of your village, town or city)* either. For a start, there are four or five camels tied up outside the door. That's not normal for *(name of place)*, is it? No, this is Jerusalem.

(The music gets louder.)

Now imagine. We're followers of Jesus, about 120 of us, all huddled together in an upstairs room. Suddenly what sounds like a tornado sweeps through.

(Sound of rushing wind)

Then what looks like a roaring fire appears from nowhere and separates into kind of flames above the head of each of us.

(Sound of crackling flames)

There are crowds outside.

(Sound of crowds chattering away excitedly)

They have piled into Jerusalem from all around the Mediterranean region. They soon discover that something amazing is happening. We're speaking in lots of different languages (How did that happen?), and whichever part of the world the crowds are from, everyone understands what we're saying! What is going on?

Don't you remember? Hundreds of years ago the prophet Joel told us God's words. He said, 'I'll pour out my Spirit on everyone.' That's what he has done! God has poured out the Holy Spirit, and with it the ripples of the good news of Jesus begin to spread.

(End of the soundtrack)

To where all the crowds come from – Parthia, Media and Elam, Mesopotamia, Judea and Cappadocia, Pontus and Asia, Phrygia and Pamphylia, Egypt and the parts of Libya near Cyrene, Rome, Crete and Arabia.

And as the crowds in Jerusalem return home, perhaps they will talk excitedly tonight about all they have seen and heard there. And maybe for some of them, about what they now believe. The ripples are spreading.

13 Man on a mission
Paul

Acts 13,14

The good news of Jesus spread in pretty unlikely ways, through some pretty unlikely people such as Saul (who became Paul), the persecutor of some of the first Christians. But the message remained the same: 'Each one of you must turn away from your sins and be baptised in the name of Jesus Christ, so that your sins will be forgiven; and you will receive God's gift, the Holy Spirit. For God's promise was made to you and your children, and to all who are far away – all whom the Lord our God calls to himself' (Acts 2:38,39 GNB).

Through signs, wonders and words of truth from God, the number of believers grew – 3,000 on the day of Pentecost itself after Peter the apostle's address to the crowd (Acts 2:41), and more and more as the praising, praying, bread-breaking fledgling church gained confidence.

This session we focus on just one of Paul's missionary journeys, because it captures the challenging situation facing the first Christians, but also the relentless empowering of the Holy Spirit that would enable God's people to fulfil what he promised Abram: 'All peoples on earth will be blessed through you' (Genesis 12:3).

Pray that, as a result of these Multi-Sensory Bible sessions, God will sweep your group along in the Spirit so that they become gospel communicators who can't help but spread the good news (1 Corinthians 9:16).

 Getting connected

Bible Timeline

Over refreshments, encourage everyone to share any discoveries from their journals. Hopefully this will by now be a natural part of how you encourage and build one another up.

Also, display the four parts of the Bible timeline all stuck together in one strip. Connect God's promise to Abram (Genesis 12:3) with the unfolding story of God and his people. Bring out some of the Multi-Sensory Bible themes – God creates, provides, shapes and leads, forgives, saves/rescues, judges, promises, and reveals who he is – and relate them to individual group members' stories, if possible.

OR

Cranium

You will need: a Cranium game (by Hasbro).

Plan a game of Cranium, splitting your group into two or three teams. Introduce into the packs, not too far down, a Creative Cat card saying 'good news', a Word Worm (Zelpuz) card with the jumbled word 'lisvnaato' ('salvation') with the clue 'gained but not earned', and Star Performer 'evangelist'. Use the usual other wording on these cards.

Living Scripture

You will need: a copy of the map on page 67 for each person, or downloaded from www.scriptureunion.org.uk/msbible; pens; Bibles.

Introduce the activity with these words:

The story since last time: After the coming of the Holy Spirit, the good news about Jesus spread in some pretty strange ways! Saul was a Pharisee, a strict Jewish leader who tried to keep every detail of the laws God gave to Moses. He hated Jesus' followers and hunted them down. As he was travelling to Damascus to persecute another group of followers, Jesus spoke to him – and Saul ended up wanting to tell everyone about Jesus! His name was changed to Paul. From then on, instead of thrashing people for following Jesus, he suffered hardship and persecution himself as he travelled three times round the Mediterranean region, helping people to get to know God. We'll trace his first journey.

Divide the group into pairs, give everyone a copy of the map, and make sure they have a pen and a Bible between them. One of each pair will trace Paul's route on the map and the other will find the Bible verses.

The Bible reader in each pair should read out the whole of Acts chapters 13 and 14, while the other draws Paul's route on the map and notes in the box beside each place what God did there to spread the gospel. The pairs may need to stop and discuss together occasionally.

When everyone has finished, they should compare notes with another pair. If there are significant differences, they should return to the Bible verses to check what they actually say.

Ask the group if they can see any of the Multi-Sensory Bible themes coming through in these two chapters. Which other parts of the Bible story might these two chapters connect with?

 Touching God

Blowing sin away
You will need: talcum powder; a Bible.

The Bible speaks of clouds as a reminder of God's presence and power, but read out Isaiah 44:22. God has the power to blow our sins away as though they were clouds.

Appoint an adjudicator to judge how far away the 'clouds' are blown. Place some talcum powder in the hand of all other group leaders. One at a time, invite them to blow their 'cloud' as far as they can. The adjudicator can find a clever way to measure the furthest point each 'cloud' reaches.

Once God has swept our sins away, they are gone for ever – forgiven and forgotten. Repeat the activity, but this time, as everyone blows, invite them to confess their sin silently.

Pass the parcel

You will need: lively music on CD or MP3 to play; a parcel made of many layers, with some top-quality chocolate in the centre, and a label saying 'Good news! You've won!'; subsequent layers with a prize for the person who opens it along with a forfeit for the person to their left ('Good news – you've won a prize, but the person to your left has to…').

Form a circle and play the game in the usual way. Make a big thing of the opening of the parcel each time, congratulating the person who gets the prize and commiserating with the person who has to do the forfeit. The same message can be good or bad news for those who hear it.

When the game is finished, get everyone to pray for the person to their right, that God will work through them to draw others to himself.

 Reaching out

You will need: a large-scale street map of your area where most of your group live; tea lights; matches.

Gather round the map. Give everyone three or four tea lights. Encourage them to choose a particular street to pray for. They should light a tea light and place it on a map over that street or road. (Take safety precautions, especially watching that group members don't lean over the tea lights.) As they do so, they should pray silently or out loud that the good news of Jesus will reach into the homes there. They could use a phrase such as 'May the light and the love of Jesus reach into (the name of the street or road).' Get people to start with the street or road where they live.

 Digging deeper

You will need: copies of the resource sheet on page 10 or downloaded from www.scriptureunion. org.uk/msbible.

Distribute the sheets. Encourage everyone as usual to reflect with their Multi-Sensory Bible journal after your session, focusing on Acts 13 and 14. Then ask them to prepare a short testimony for next time, covering how they first heard about Jesus and took the step to follow him. What was good news to them about what they heard or experienced?

Big story

Encourage group members to focus again on Acts 13:16–41 and note each of the Bible incidents Paul mentions. They should then try to work out why he chose those particular incidents to communicate the gospel to the Jewish people in Antioch of Pisidia. History has been heading somewhere special, he said.

Bible timeline Part 4

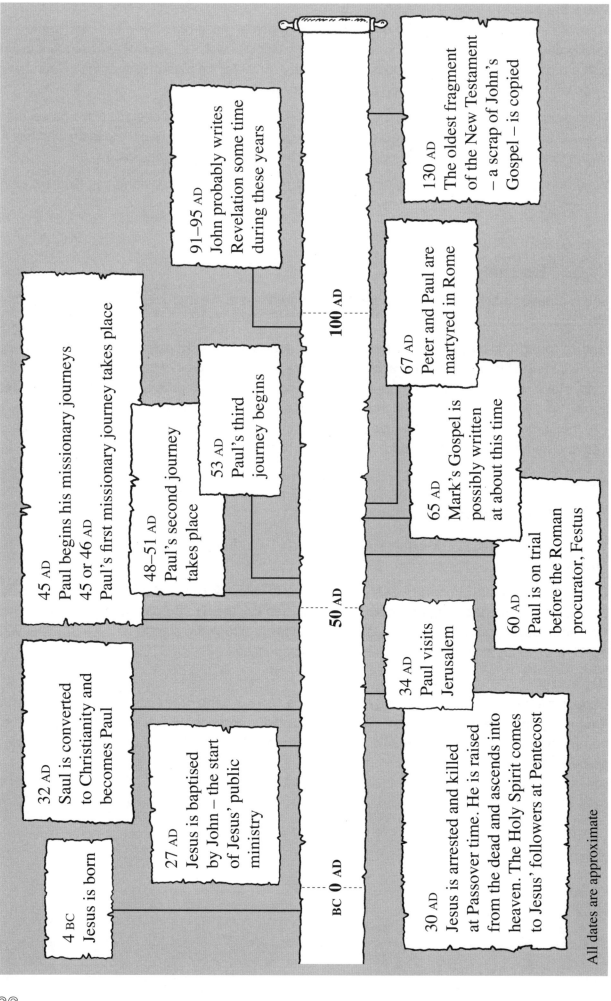

4 BC
Jesus is born

27 AD
Jesus is baptised by John – the start of Jesus' public ministry

32 AD
Saul is converted to Christianity and becomes Paul

45 AD
Paul begins his missionary journeys

45 or 46 AD
Paul's first missionary journey takes place

48–51 AD
Paul's second journey takes place

53 AD
Paul's third journey begins

91–95 AD
John probably writes Revelation some time during these years

130 AD
The oldest fragment of the New Testament – a scrap of John's Gospel – is copied

67 AD
Peter and Paul are martyred in Rome

65 AD
Mark's Gospel is possibly written at about this time

60 AD
Paul is on trial before the Roman procurator, Festus

34 AD
Paul visits Jerusalem

30 AD
Jesus is arrested and killed at Passover time. He is raised from the dead and ascends into heaven. The Holy Spirit comes to Jesus' followers at Pentecost

BC 0 AD

50 AD

100 AD

All dates are approximate

Paul's first journey

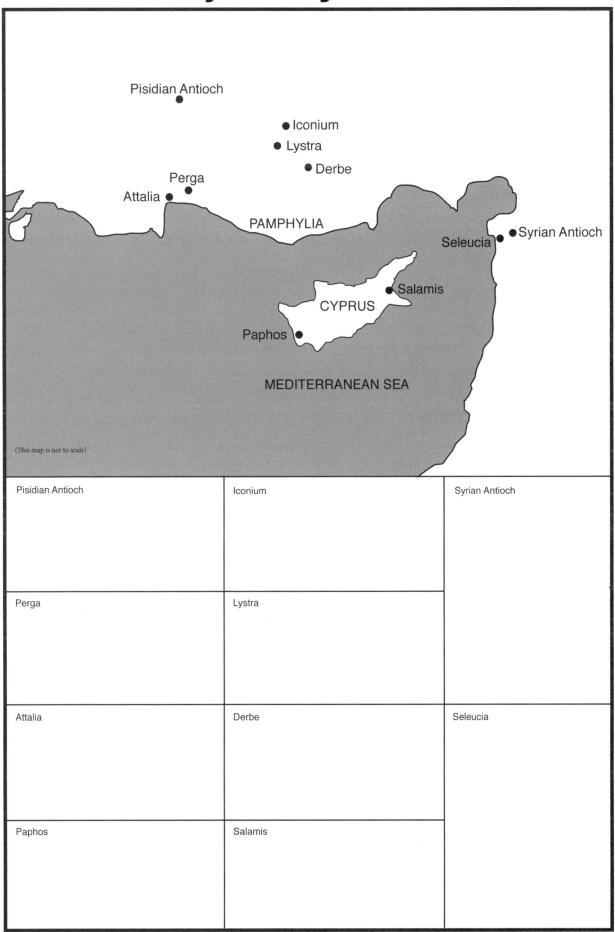

Pisidian Antioch
●

● Iconium

● Lystra

● Derbe

Perga
●

Attalia ●

PAMPHYLIA

Seleucia ● ● Syrian Antioch

● Salamis

CYPRUS

Paphos ●

MEDITERRANEAN SEA

(This map is not to scale)

Pisidian Antioch	Iconium	Syrian Antioch
Perga	Lystra	
Attalia	Derbe	Seleucia
Paphos	Salamis	

14 Solid foundations
The early church

Matthew 7:24–27; Ephesians 2:11–22; Colossians 2:6,7

'Apostles' were those who had been commissioned by Jesus as his witnesses – the twelve – though Saul/Paul called himself an 'apostle' too, because Jesus appeared to him on the road to Damascus. Others in the early church were known as apostles as well, often as those to whom Jesus appeared after his resurrection.

'Apostle' means 'sent' – those Jesus sent out to spread his teachings. The important thing for the early church was to keep as close a contact with Jesus as possible, even after he had gone back to heaven. Jesus was the 'foundation' of their faith. So the apostles were very highly respected.

Often, in the New Testament letters to the various churches, Christians are warned to get back to the foundations or roots of their faith, Jesus, as the sure way to withstand all that the world (and Satan) could throw at them. As the message spread, it was important to stay in touch with the truth as seen and heard in Jesus, rather than 'wobbling' unsteadily by believing any passing, whimsical teaching. In this session your group will experience two such Bible passages.

Pray that your group will feel free to share about their experience of coming to faith in Jesus, and will be strengthened in their determination to say close to him all their lives.

 Getting connected

Telling stories
You will need: celebratory food such as cup cakes, doughnuts or a party slab.

Over drinks and a celebratory bite to eat, encourage everyone to tell their story about how they first heard the good news of Jesus and took the step to follow him. What was the good news to them? Invite everyone else to ask questions of the person speaking, unless you think it will be too threatening for them.

OR

Wise and foolish builders
You will need: the video of 'The wise and foolish builders' – you'll find a link on our website: www.scriptureunion.org.uk/msbible; something to show it on; Bibles.

Sit back and enjoy this lovely cartoon of Jesus' parable. Since there is no spoken language on the video, it would be good to play it once or twice more, inviting two group members each time to speak out the thoughts of the two characters like a voiceover as the video plays. If they're not sure, a quick glance at Matthew 7:24–27 will help.

Living Scripture

You will need: copies of the resource sheet on page 71, or downloaded from www.scriptureunion. org.uk/msbible; Bibles; pens; reflective background music.

Introduce this activity with the following words:

The story since last time: The church grew and grew. So that there was no Chinese Whispers effect as the good news was passed on, or no deliberate attempt to deceive, Christians in the early church were often warned to go back to the original source, Jesus, the 'foundation' of the faith. This was especially important when false teachers were in town. We zoom in on the small Christian church in Ephesus.

Turn to Ephesians chapter 1 verses 1 and 2. Who is the letter addressed to? 'Saints'. That describes us – all God's people. 'Faithful'. That's us too – full of faith in God. 'In Christ Jesus'. Certainly – in the closest possible relationship with Jesus, as intimately attached as branches are to the vine. 'In Ephesus'. That's not us exactly! But we do live in a place that's just as full of distractions away from the One True God.

Divide your group into pairs or threes, and give each pair or three a resource sheet. Make sure they have a pen and Bible between them.

Allow everyone 20 minutes or so to work through the sheet individually, as the music plays. Then invite two of the pairs or threes to get together to compare their answers. Finally draw everyone back together to share their findings.

What is their overwhelming discovery about these verses?

 Touching God

'Overflowing with thankfulness'
You will need: marker pens; three large sheets of paper with one of each of the words 'Christ', 'Jesus' and 'Lord' written in the middle of them; Bibles; ambient music.

Read Colossians 2:6,7 together. The names and titles used to describe the One on whom our faith is built are not randomly or casually chosen – 'Christ', 'Jesus', 'Lord'. Underneath each of the words on the large sheet, note a few words or phrases to remind everyone what the names signify:

'Christ' – the One chosen by God, the promised Messiah who was expected to rescue God's people

'Jesus' – the Saviour who came to earth to meet our deepest need, to die like a criminal to take away the guilt for sin that is rightly ours

'Lord' – the God of his people Israel, the One who is greater than any other and demands our all

Spread out the three sheets on the floor or stick them to the walls. Play ambient music and invite everyone to take marker pens and write short phrases of prayer, praise or thankfulness based on the name or title and description on each sheet.

Roots

You will need: a printout of the two pictures and the prayer at www.scriptureunion.org.uk/msbible; Bibles.

Show the picture of the tree and ask if anyone knows what it is. It's the Mendocino Tree, a coast redwood in California, the tallest tree in the world at around 112 metres and 1,000 years old. Ask why they think the tree hasn't simply fallen over before now.

Show the picture of the tower and ask everyone what it is. It's the Leaning Tower of Pisa, in Northern Italy. The problem with it is that the craftsmen who started to build it in 1173 only laid a foundation that was three metres deep. The tower is 54.5 metres high. It began to subside immediately. When it was completed 200 years later, it was still subsiding, and it's getting harder and harder for engineers to stop it falling over completely. The foundations are the problem.

Read Colossians 2:6,7 together. Even though Paul had never been to Colossae, he knew that he and the Christians there had something in common – a firm faith in the Lord Jesus. When people tried to tell the Colossians things about God that weren't true, Paul warned them to stick with what Jesus taught and the way Jesus lived, and follow him. Jesus was to be the solid foundation of their life.

Get everyone to clasp their hands tightly together with overlapping fingers. Lead them in the prayer, asking them to repeat each line after you.

 ## Reaching out

The early church, as described in Acts 2:42–47, was remarkable and compelling just by what they did and where they did it, because God was at work in and through them. 'Teaching', 'fellowship', 'breaking of bread', 'prayer', 'wonders and signs', shared possessions and meals, 'praising God' – let this list stimulate your group's thoughts about how it might best connect with the community around it.

 ## Digging deeper

Multi-Sensory journals – last time!
You will need: copies of the resource sheet on page 10 or downloaded from www.scriptureunion.org.uk/msbible.

Encourage everyone to do their Multi-Sensory Bible journaling with this session's passages – it's probably the last time ever!

Days
Challenge everyone to take one photo a day on their mobile to represent any of the Multi-Sensory Bible themes. Next session, invite everyone to share their photos, maybe uploaded to your Facebook page.

BUILD ON HIM

1 From these verses, say who has achieved all that has been done.

. . . .

. . . .

. . . .

. . . .

. . . .

. . . .

. . . .

2 From these verses, in the 'Before' column, list all the ways of describing Gentiles (non-Jews) before Jesus came. In the 'After' column, describe them afterwards.

Before . . . .

. . . .

. . . .

. . . .

. . . .

After . . . .

. . . .

. . . .

. . . .

. . . .

3 All this God has freely given to us – we couldn't earn it or make it happen for ourselves. Pause to thank him for Jesus. Note one or two phrases of thanks that you use.

. . . .

. . . .

. . . .

. . . .

. . . .

. . . .

Ephesians 2:11–22, NIV

[11] Therefore, remember that formerly you who are Gentiles by birth and called 'uncircumcised' by those who call themselves 'the circumcision' (which is done in the body by human hands) – [12] remember that at that time you were separate from Christ, excluded from citizenship in Israel and foreigners to the covenants of the promise, without hope and without God in the world. [13] But now in Christ Jesus you who once were far away have been brought near by the blood of Christ.

[14] For he himself is our peace, who has made the two groups one and has destroyed the barrier, the dividing wall of hostility, [15] by setting aside in his flesh the law with its commands and regulations. His purpose was to create in himself one new humanity out of the two, thus making peace, [16] and in one body to reconcile both of them to God through the cross, by which he put to death their hostility. [17] He came and preached peace to you who were far away and peace to those who were near. [18] For through him we both have access to the Father by one Spirit.

[19] Consequently, you are no longer foreigners and strangers, but fellow citizens with God's people and also members of his household, [20] built on the foundation of the apostles and prophets, with Christ Jesus himself as the chief cornerstone. [21] In him the whole building is joined together and rises to become a holy temple in the Lord. [22] And in him you too are being built together to become a dwelling in which God lives by his Spirit.

4 How does this relate to the story of your own coming to faith? How is your 'before' and 'after' reflected in these verses?

. . . .

. . . .

. . . .

. . . .

. . . .

. . . .

. . . .

5 Underline any words or phrases that particularly strike you. Why do they?

. . . .

. . . .

. . . .

. . . .

. . . .

. . . .

. . . .

6 How do the last few verses describe what the Christian's role is in life?

. . . .

. . . .

. . . .

. . . .

. . . .

. . . .

15 Totally glorious!

Jesus' return

Isaiah 65:17–25; 2 Peter 3:3–15; Revelation 21,22

Sometimes the Christian life can be a struggle – perhaps even most of the time. We wonder why it should be if we believe and trust in Jesus, and he is the Lord of all and our best friend. The reason is that we are in the in-between times – Jesus has died for us, we have been saved, but we are still becoming all that God wants us to be, and the world is still groaning as it waits for Jesus' return and the creation of a new heaven and earth. We know the final chapter of the story with no end – the outcome is certain – but we just haven't got there yet.

Old Testament prophets had spoken of a decisive 'day of the Lord', when God would judge nations but also renew his people (for example, Ezekiel 36:24–28), creating a new heaven and earth (for example, Isaiah 32:14–20). In the New Testament, this 'day' is the time when Jesus returns (for example, 1 Corinthians 1:8 and Philippians 1:6). And the new heaven and earth will be utterly glorious – Revelation 21 and 22 certainly whet our appetite.

Pray that your group members will be able to understand the future we're heading for in the Lord, and their need to work towards the time when Jesus returns and God's kingdom will be fully revealed in him.

 Getting connected

Discoveries

Over refreshments, ask if anyone is willing to share their journaling discoveries since last time, and maybe also show their daily theme photos (see 'Days' page 70).

If you have time, encourage all those who have been journaling to share what the value of it has been to them. The idea was that it should help them see God at work in their lives and discover their own place in God's big story. Did that actually happen for anyone?

OR

Pray about any major discoveries that group members have made all the time they have been doing their Multi-Sensory Bible journaling.

Hidden, revealed

You will need: ten uniquely shaped household objects, such as a sieve, a vase, a photo frame etc; ten tea towels; pens; paper.

Before the group arrives, completely cover each item with a tea towel. Arrange them on the floor or table in the middle of where the group will sit.

Give each person a pen and sheet of paper and ask them to guess what the items are. Reveal them one by one as individuals mark each other's sheets.

What is hidden will be revealed. God's kingdom is largely unseen, but one day it will be clearly revealed, when Jesus returns.

Living Scripture

You will need: Bibles.

Set the scene in this way:

The story since last time: The church has grown and grown, but it's not all plain sailing. In fact, it's suffering from deceptive teachers, bad relationships, and persecution from the Roman authorities. Things weren't meant to be like this, surely! The prophet Isaiah knew that, in the future, God's kingdom would come on earth – the whole of creation would be renewed, with a new heaven and new earth like the Garden of Eden – a new 'birth' that would encompass everything.

Together read Isaiah 65:17–25 and 66:22. Decide how you would direct these scenes if you were making a film. Start with chapter 65, verse 17. What do you see? Close, medium or long shot? What would you focus on? How would the words be spoken – joyfully, sorrowfully, reflectively, urgently…? Break up the scenes like this: verses 18/19/20, 21/22/23/24/25.

If you were God's chosen people back then, what would you want to say to him about this?

Now read 2 Peter 3:3–13, pausing at the end of each verse to let what has been said sink in.

The New Testament makes it clear that, first, Jesus will return to sort out those who trust in him and those who don't; then God will create the new heaven and earth. Simply enjoy hearing two people read Revelation 21 and 22, a chapter each.

What are the similarities and differences between this wonderful place and the Garden of Eden?

Christians have a secure place in the new heaven and earth, where we have always longed to be, the ultimate experience of God's kingdom. There the covenant will be kept in the best possible way (v 3). Praise the Lord!

 Touching God

Foretaste

You will need: a copy of the resource sheet on page 75 for each person or downloaded from www.scriptureunion.org.uk/msbible; ambient music.

Cut up a set of slips for each person. They illustrate aspects of life that will no longer be present in the new heaven and earth (Revelation 21,22).

Play the music. Hand out the slips of paper and invite everyone to write on each slip something that is going on in their lives or in the world at large related to that aspect of life.

When everyone has finished, say, 'Of all these things there will be no more in the new heaven and earth.' Get everyone to tear all their slips into small pieces and throw them in the air. Praise God!

Precious gems

You will need: a pack of beautiful artificial gems, available cheaply online – see the suggested link at www.scriptureunion.org.uk/msbible (alternatively use any real jewellery with gems that you may have); Bibles; ambient music.

Play the music. Give each person an artificial gem stone, or two or three if you have enough. Encourage them to look closely as the light is reflected and refracted in them. Imagine a bride dressed entirely in gems, with light shining out from within. Enjoy the beauty. They may wish to read again Revelation 21:9–21.

'The bride, the wife of the Lamb' is the church (Revelation 21:9). Reflect on what you see in the church and in yourself that is 'beautiful' – and becoming more so – in God's scheme of things. Thank him for it silently and pray that it will become even more so.

 Reaching out

As you finish these sessions, arrange a date for a meal together in two or three months' time. When you get to it, chat together about anything that has particularly stuck with you from your Multi-Sensory Bible experience. Make sure you comment about it on the group's Facebook page, and take some photos.

 Digging deeper

All together now!

You will need: the pieces of the Bible story from A3 copies of pages 76 to 78, or downloaded and printed from www.scriptureunion.org.uk/msbible.

Shuffle and distribute the pieces like playing cards around your group members. Challenge them as a whole team to lay out on the floor the complete Bible story, with all the pieces in the right order. Everyone must be responsible for putting down their own pieces rather than one person collecting them up and doing all the work.

If they have them all in the correct order, the letters on the sheets should read: 'God's dwelling-place is now among the people, and he will dwell with them...' (Revelation 21:3).

Explain how this moment in this verse is what the whole story of everything has been leading to – God living as close as possible to his people for ever. Also, indicate where the present moment in time is located, before Jesus' return, and help your group to look forward to all that is still to come.

The Bible in 50 words

You will need: copies of the resource sheet on page 19 or downloaded from www.scriptureunion. org.uk/msbible.

Using all the phrases of 'The Bible in 50 words', have fun getting your group to learn the whole story by heart. Maybe break it down first so that each person reads one phrase and you recite it round the group.

Foretaste

Tears	
....	

Death	
....	

Mourning	
....	

Crying	
....	

Evil	
....	

Sun and moon	
....	

Night	
....	

Impurity	
....	

Deceit	
....	

Shamefulness	
....	

Distance between God and his people	
....	

All Together NOW!

G	God creates the universe, with people as the best of creation.
O	People choose to disobey God and are separated from him.
D	People become 'civilised' and try to live without God.
S	In a flood God wipes out all living things, except Noah and his family.
H	God tells Abram to set out for the land that God will show him. Abram obeys.
O	Abram arrives in Canaan, the Promised Land.
M	God changes Abram's name to Abraham, meaning 'father of many nations' – the beginning of the first covenant (agreement) with his people.
E	Abraham's son Isaac lives in Canaan as a shepherd.
I	Abraham's grandson Jacob lives in Canaan with his twelve sons.
S	Famine hits Canaan. There's not enough food for Jacob's large family.
N	Jacob's family moves to Egypt where one of the sons, Joseph, is in charge of the corn supplies.
O	Jacob's descendants live in Egypt for four hundred years. They become slaves to the Egyptians.
W	God makes Jacob's descendants into a nation, the people of Israel. 'Israel' is another name for Jacob.
W	God sends Moses to get his people out of Egypt.

I	God gives them the Ten Commandments and other rules for living. Now they really are his people.
T	Israel enters into a covenant with God. They are his people and he will protect them, so they promise to obey him.
H	The Israelites cross the River Jordan with Joshua as their leader, and enter Canaan, their Promised Land.
H	Hostile tribes in Canaan try to get rid of the Israelites.
I	The Israelites settle in Canaan.
S	God gives the Israelites judges to help them fight against the tribes that are already in Canaan. Most judges are soldiers.
P	The last judge is Samuel, not a soldier but a prophet, someone who tells God's people what he wants them to know.
E	The people say they want a king. Samuel reminds them that God is their king, so they don't need any other.
O	God lets the Israelites have a king, Saul.
P	After Saul, Israel has two brilliant kings – David, then his son Solomon.
L	During Solomon's reign, Israel enjoys peace and prosperity like never before.
E	Solomon's son Rehoboam is a harsh king. Only two tribes of Israelites (Benjamin and Judah) want him as king. The other ten ask for Jeroboam, who was one of Solomon's officials.
H	Israel splits in two. The northern half of the country is now called Israel. The southern half is called Judah.
E	Then in both Israel and Judah there is a series of kings and a queen. A few of them obey God, but most of them don't.
W	The Assyrians attack Israel and take the people captive.

I	The Babylonians attack Judah, destroy Jerusalem and take God's people captive into Babylonia.
L	The Persians release God's people from Babylonia. Many return to Jerusalem to rebuild the walls and temple. They wait for God's chosen king.
L	Around four hundred years later, Jesus is born to save people from the wrong that separates them from God.
L	Jesus teaches and heals, telling and showing people the good news of God's kingdom.
I	Jesus dies, so that everyone can become one of God's people.
V	God raises Jesus from death. The good news of Jesus is for everyone.
E	Jesus returns to heaven.
W	God sends the Holy Spirit to help Jesus' followers. The church is born.
I	Saul, a Pharisee, arrests Jesus' followers and throws them in prison.
T	Saul himself becomes a follower of Jesus and is called Paul instead.
H	Paul travels three times round the Mediterranean lands with the good news of Jesus.
T	More and more people trust Jesus. But the Romans make life hard for Christians, and kill some of them.
H	Today the number of God's people is still growing.
E	One day Jesus will return.
M	God will make a new heaven and a new earth, and all his people will be with him in heaven, as close to him as possible.

Other books in the Multi-Sensory series

✳ fresh ✳ innovative ✳ imaginative ✳ inspirational ✳ practical

MULTI-SENSORY CHURCH

Over 30 ready-to-use ideas for creative churches and small groups

Sue Wallace

MULTI-SENSORY SCRIPTURE

50 innovative ideas for exploring the Bible in churches and small groups

Sue Wallace

MULTI-SENSORY MESSAGE

Ready-to-use Bible-based activities on mission – for creative churches and small groups

Dave Maclure

MULTI-SENSORY SEASONS

15 ready-to-use Bible-based sessions through the seasons for creative small groups

Wendy Rayner and Annie Slade

MULTI-SENSORY PARABLES

15 ready-to-use sessions on the stories Jesus told – for creative churches and small groups

Ian Birkinshaw

MULTI-SENSORY TOGETHER

15 ready-to-use sessions for Bible exploration in creative small groups

Ian Birkinshaw

MULTI-SENSORY PRAYER

Over 60 ready-to-use ideas for creative churches and small groups

Sue Wallace

MULTI-SENSORY WORLD

Global issues explored – for creative churches, youth groups and small groups

Craig Borlase

MULTI-SENSORY PROPHETS

15 ready-to-use sessions on God's messengers – for creative churches and small groups

Mike Law

MULTI-SENSORY WORSHIP

Over 60 ready-to-use prayer activities for creative churches

Sue Wallace

This series is just part of a wide range of resources for churches and small groups published by Scripture Union.

SU publications are available from Christian bookshops, on the Internet or via mail order.
You can:

✳   Phone SU's mail order line: 0845 0706006

✳   Email info@scriptureunion.org.uk

✳   Log on to www.scriptureunion.org.uk

✳   Write to SU Mail Order, PO Box 5148, Milton Keynes MLO, MK2 2YX